MW00331944

Project Management and Organizational Change

*Lynn Crawford, DBA, Human Systems International
Limited and Bond University, Australia*
Alicia Aitken, PhD, Human Systems International Limited
Anat Hassner-Nahmias, PhD, Krusner Pty Ltd

ISBN: 978-1-62825-043-5

Published by: Project Management Institute, Inc.
14 Campus Boulevard
Newtown Square, Pennsylvania 19073-3299 USA
Phone: +610-356-4600
Fax: +610-356-4647
Email: customercare@pmi.org
Internet: www.PMI.org

©2014 Project Management Institute, Inc. All rights reserved.

Cover design by David Riedy
Cover image (c) hakkiarslan/iStockphoto

"PMI", the PMI logo, "PMP", the PMP logo, "PMBOK", "PgMP", "Project Management Journal",
"PM Network", and the PMI Today logo are registered marks of Project Management Institute, Inc.
The Quarter Globe Design is a trademark of the Project Management Institute, Inc. For a comprehensive list of PMI marks, contact the PMI Legal Department.

PMI Publications welcomes corrections and comments on its books. Please feel free to send comments on typographical, formatting, or other errors. Simply make a copy of the relevant page of the book, mark the error, and send it to: Book Editor, PMI Publications, 14 Campus Boulevard, Newtown Square, PA 19073-3299 USA.

To inquire about discounts for resale or educational purposes, please contact the PMI Book Service Center.

PMI Book Service Center
P.O. Box 932683, Atlanta, GA 31193-2683 USA
Phone: 1-866-276-4764 (within the U.S. or Canada) or +1-770-280-4129 (globally)
Fax: +1-770-280-4113
Email: info@bookorders.pmi.org

Printed in the United States of America. No part of this work may be reproduced or transmitted in any form or by any means, electronic, manual, photocopying, recording, or by any information storage and retrieval system, without prior written permission of the publisher.

The paper used in this book complies with the Permanent Paper Standard issued by the National Information Standards Organization (Z39.48—1984).

10 9 8 7 6 5 4 3 2 1

Acknowledgments

The authors wish to thank the individuals and organizations that participated in this research for their time and effort and acknowledge the support provided by the Project Management Institute's Research Department and by the authors' employing organizations: Bond University, Australia, Human Systems International Limited, and Presence of IT.

Executive Summary

Organizational changes have become recognized as a distinct type of project or program, and it may be argued that the majority of projects involve some degree of organizational and behavioral change. The degree of this change can be expected to be greater in projects where the purpose is to achieve organizational change, but even where the focus is on other outcomes, achievement of desired benefits may require structural changes and will generally involve some change in the way people do things. However, while project managers claim to be implementers of change, current project management standards focus on change control but largely ignore the complex and emergent characteristics associated with implementation of change that is necessary to deliver value.

This report presents results of a quantitative research study undertaken in response to a request from the Project Management Institute, through their research program, for proposals to investigate the relationship between project management and organizational change. The primary aim of the study was to identify the nature of practices used by those in project, program, and change roles in managing projects requiring varying degrees of organizational and behavioral change.

From a project management perspective, a major finding of this research is that those in project roles appear to be embracing change implementation practices, despite their absence from the main project management standards for both knowledge and performance. Change implementation practices are being used by project management practitioners across a range of projects independent of degree of organizational and behavioral change and industry sector. All project, program, and change implementation practices were found to be associated with the success of projects, but those practices found to be the strongest predictors of likelihood of project success are drawn from the change implementation toolkit: making informed decisions and ensuring business integration. Notably, those who hold some form of project management professional certification appear to be more likely to use higher levels of business integration practice.

Table of Contents

List of Figures and Tables

Chapter 1

Introduction

Background

Organizational changes have become recognized as a distinct type of project or program that is generating a growing research interest within the project management field (Crawford & Hassner-Nahmias, 2010). As Söderlund (2010, p. 131) observed, change is increasingly being organized as projects and projects in general, whether development or business projects, are increasingly involving change elements. Further, project managers claim to be agents and managers of change (Turner, Grude, & Thurloway, 1996; Association for Project Management [APM], 2006) and the effective management of such change has been recognized as a factor contributing to project success (Tan, Cater-Steel, & Toleman, 2009; Nicholas & Hidding, 2010; Levasseur, 2010; Martin, 2011).

Recognition of the changes necessitated by projects is not new. Some 20 years ago, Buchanan (1991, p. 122) pointed out that it was uncommon to find an organization introducing technical changes unaccompanied by changes to manufacturing systems and administrative procedures. A search of the subsequent project management journal literature will find some research and practice articles that deal with aspects of organizational change being managed as projects or programs (e.g., Partington, 1996; Levene & Braganza, 1996; Pellegrinelli, 1997; Cicmil, 1999a; Crawford, Costello, Pollack, & Bentley, 2003; Leybourne, 2006; Lehtonen & Martinsuo, 2008; Nieminen & Lehtonen, 2008; Gareis, 2010).

To date, however, management of organizational change has continued to have a relatively small representation in the project management literature. Also, although project and program management standards address communications and stakeholder management, and these are important in the management of change, the standards do not specifically address the knowledge and skills required to manage organizational and behavioral change as identified in change management literature and standards (Hassner-Nahmias & Crawford, 2008).

By contrast, organizational change management is a central concern of the organizational behavior and development literature. Here, the role of the change manager, usually with an organizational change and/or development background, is now well established, although its support as a profession lags significantly behind that of the project management profession.

With few exceptions (Leybourne, 2006, 2007), there is little connection between the project management and change management literatures (Bresnen, 2006; Gareis & Huemann, 2008; Lehmann, 2010), and two distinct bodies of knowledge underpin the practices of the project manager and the change manager (Crawford & Hassner-Nahmias, 2010). Nevertheless, there is some recognition in the change management literature that more effective implementation of change may be achieved through application of project management approaches (Whittington, Molloy, Mayer, & Smith, 2006; Lehmann, 2010) and that managers of organizational change projects need project management skills (Dover, 2003; Leybourne, 2006; Biedenbach & Söderholm, 2008; Oswick & Robertson, 2009).

There is, however, considerable lack of clarity concerning the relationship between change, project, and program roles (Stummer & Zuchi, 2010), and in the project management field, there are two quite different interpretations of the term "change management." Change managers use the term "change management" to refer to implementation of necessary or desirable change primarily to structure, processes, and behaviors, but for project managers, the established use of the term relates to processes for change control.

Griffith-Cooper and King (2007) distinguish between change control, focusing on project scope, schedule, cost, quality, risk, and procurement, and change leadership, which "promotes project success by guiding those affected by the project through the inevitable stages of human reaction to change" (p. 15). The focus of prominent project management guides, such as the *APM Body of Knowledge* (Association for Project Management [APM], 2006), *IPMA Competency Baseline* (ICB) (International Project Management Association [IPMA], 2006), and *A Guide to the Project Management Body of Knowledge (PMBOK® Guide)* (Project Management Institute [PMI], 2008a), is on change control. The term "change management" is used but primarily in the sense of "the formal process through which changes to the project plan are approved and introduced" (APM, 2006, p. 130), which "helps to keep track of changes in the scope as well as in the configuration of the project" (PMI, 2008a, p. 60).

The *Glossary of Project Management Terms* (APM, 2006) acknowledges that the term "change management" may also be used to refer to a process whereby organizational change is introduced. All three standards (APM, IPMA, and PMI) suggest, however, that the introduction of organizational change is the province of program or line management rather than the project: "If the project concerns organizational change, then the change to be implemented as an outcome of the project is managed by line management, not by the project team" (IPMA, 2006, p. 16). The *PMBOK®*

Guide (PMI, 2008a) states that change is something that the program manager must expect and be prepared to manage.

To avoid confusion between the meaning of change management as either change control or introduction of desirable change, we have adopted the term "change implementation" in referring to processes whereby required or desirable change is introduced.

Research Aims

The Project Management Institute, recognizing that organizational change has existed for a long time as a specialized field in general management that is largely independent of the field of project management, requested proposals for research to examine and further investigate organizational change. The research presented in this report is a response to this request. Although the research encompasses both project management and change implementation and aims to enhance the connection between the two, the starting point and expected primary audience is the project management field.

Expected contributions from the research are enrichment of the theoretical underpinnings of project and program management; contribution to practice in project management and change implementation fields; opportunities for cross-fertilization between project management and change management/organizational development research and literature; and a direct contribution to the body of knowledge and standards in project and program management.

In particular, the research was designed to identify:

a. the nature of organizational and behavioral change related activities associated with the management of projects/programs;
b. the nature of project/program management related activities associated with the management of organizational change projects;
c. the extent to which such activities vary relative to the type of project/program, context, and degree of organizational and behavioral change involved; and
d. patterns of relative involvement of those with project management, organizational development, and other backgrounds in the management of organizational change projects and the organizational and behavioral change related activities associated with projects.

Investigation was not limited to projects considered to be organizational change projects but encompassed all projects on the assumption that the majority involve some degree of organizational and/or behavioral change. This approach was supported by research that suggests that the success of projects could be enhanced by increased attention to human factors (Buchanan & Boddy, 1992; By, 2005; Luo, Hilty, Worley, & Yager, 2006; Maguire & Redman, 2007).

Underlying Assumptions

The expected contribution was guided by these following assumptions:

- There is considerable literature relating to organizational development and change but little if any connection between this and the project management literature.
- Theory and practice in both project management and organizational change would benefit from enhanced understanding and development of the relationship between them.
- The majority of projects involve some degree of behavioral and/or organizational change.
- The importance of ability to manage behavioral and/or organizational change is not well or overtly recognized in the project management literature, standards, or certification.
- Change management related activities may be undertaken by a project, program, or change manager.
- There is often, in practice, no clear or consistent distinction made between use of the terms "project" and "program" (this assumption is based on recent experience of the researchers).
- A higher degree of required behavioral and/or organizational change will require a proportionately higher level of specific change management related skills.
- Use of change management related practices increases in relation to the degree of organizational and behavioral change involved.
- All change initiatives will involve some degree of behavioral change, but not all change initiatives will involve organizational change (hence, reference to behavioral and/or organizational change).
- The likelihood of project success is related to the degree of behavioral and organizational change involved (Sirkin et al., 2005).

Research Questions

These underlying assumptions were translated into these specific research questions:

Project, program, and change related practices

1. What is the nature of project, program, and change related practices associated with the management of projects?

Relationship between nature of the project, practitioner role, and background and use of project, program, and change practices

Nature of the project

2. Does use of project, program, and change related practices vary relative to the **degree of organizational and behavioral change** involved?
3. Does use of project, program, and change related practices vary between projects conducted in **public and private sector organizations**?

4. Does use of project, program, and change related practices vary between projects conducted in **finance and services and engineering sectors**?
5. Does use of project, program, and change related practices vary between projects conducted **for internal and external clients**?
6. Does use of project, program, and change related practices vary between projects of different levels of **complexity**?

Role and background of the practitioner

7. Does use of project, program, and change related practices vary according to **role**?
8. Does use of project, program, and change related practices vary between practitioners according to **age**?
9. Does use of project, program, and change related practices vary between practitioners according to **gender**?
10. Does use of project, program, and change related practices vary between practitioners with different **educational backgrounds** (PM or CM, etc.)?
11. Does use of project, program, and change related practices vary between practitioners according to length and type of **experience** (PM/CM/other)?
12. Is there a difference in levels of underpinning project management and change implementation knowledge between roles?

Finally, an interesting and important practical question is whether the use of any of these project and change related practices has an impact on the likelihood of project success. To address this, we have one more research question:

Relationship between use of project, program, and change implementation practices and project success

13. Can use of any project, program, and change related practices be identified as predictors of perceived likelihood of **project success**?

Organization of the Report

In Chapter 2, a literature review briefly addresses the key themes underpinning this research: the nature of the project and its management, including an overview of organizational and behavioral change; the concept of project success and the emergence of change implementation as a critical success factor; the role and background of the practitioner and standards for practice for project, program, and change implementation.

Chapter 3 covers the research design and methodology and introduces the data and variables available for analysis.

Chapter 4 presents the analysis of the data, and the answers this provides to the 13 research questions.

Chapter 5 summarizes the findings of the research and concludes the report.

Chapter 2

Literature Review

It is a popular view in the project management community that projects and programs are a way of organizing changes (Beidenbach & Söderholm, 2008, as cited in Gareis & Huemann, 2010, p. 311; Bresnen, 2006; Cicmil, 1999b; Lehtonen & Martinsuo, 2008; Pellegrinelli, 1997) and that project managers are managers of change or change agents (Turner et al., 1996). However, even in the project management community, management of organizational changes tends to be viewed largely as the province of program managers (PMI, 2008a), although Pellegrinelli and others (Pellegrinelli, 2002; Pellegrinelli, Partington, Hemingway, Mohdzain, & Shah, 2007) warn that program managers promoted from project management roles using conventional project management techniques are not always successful in achieving successful organizational change.

Conventional project management texts and guides take a rational-linear view with related expectation that the critical competencies of the project manager will be concerned with project control and technical expertise (Buchanan, 1991, p. 122). This approach has been challenged by the Scandinavian school of thought (Sahlin-Andersson & Söderholm, 2002) and by researchers investigating the actuality of projects and their management (Cicmil, Williams, Thomas, & Hodgson, 2006; Winter, Smith, Morris, & Cicmil, 2006). Both suggest that project managers should be engaging in activities that go beyond the traditional control agenda and, accordingly, have in their repertoire the competencies required to meet the demands of organizational change projects (Crawford & Hassner-Nahmias, 2010, p. 406). Where significant amounts of behavioral and organizational change are involved, Partington, Pelligrinelli, and Young (2005) consider that this demands high levels of interpersonal skills, astuteness, and sensitivity, as well as a fundamentally different approach to the candid, direct, and rational style valued in competent project managers. This would appear to particularly apply to projects or programs that might be characterized as involving second order change (Levy & Merry, 1986; Gareis, 2010), involving radical re-positioning or transformation.

In the change management field, the Change Management Association (www.cmassociation.org) was established in 2001 with the aim of providing a forum for change management professionals to assist and learn from each other. The Change

Management Institute (CMI) (www.change-management-institute.com) formed in Australia in 2007, has developed a Change Practitioner Competency Model and is developing an accreditation process. The CMI states that they have been motivated to develop their competency model and associated accreditation process because their research indicates that business finds "it hard to know what to look for in a Change Manager as the variety of CVs they receive when recruiting is enormous. Feedback from experienced change managers indicates frustration with comments like 'everyone thinks they are a Change Manager'. Practitioners also feel that the profession is being discredited by a lack of definition and poor quality practitioners" (www.change-management-institute.com/CMIAccreditation.aspx). This concern is reminiscent of similar concerns of the project management field in the late 20th century.

The Association for Change Management Professionals was incorporated in the District of Columbia in February 2011 as a non-profit 501(c)(6) organization. Its aims are these (Association of Change Management Professionals [ACMP], 2012):

- To expedite the recognition and growth of change management as a professional discipline;
- To develop and manage a system of professional accreditation for those engaged in various forms of managing change, enabling employers to identify qualified professionals;
- To provide affiliation, networking, education, and professional development opportunities for change management professionals; and
- To operate broadly for the benefit of the change management profession.

In February 2011, ACMP claimed to have reached 1,150 members since opening membership in May 2011, and their stated goal is to have 2,013 members in 2013. They held their inaugural conference, previously the Prosci Global Conference, in May 2011 in Orlando, FL, with 700 attendees.

It is interesting to note that there is recognition among change managers and the organizational behavior/development fields of the need of managers of organizational change projects to have project management skills. For instance, the CMI Change Practitioner Competency Model includes a unit on project management (one of 11 units or sections).

In practice, the role and professional background of the person best suited to manage organizational change initiatives is often a matter of impassioned debate. Those who come from a project management background support the view that such initiatives should be managed by a project or program manager (Kliem, Ludin, & Robertson, 1997; Obeng, 1994; Meredith & Mantel, 1995; Turner et al., 1996). Others maintain that the manager of organizational change should come from a background that is less technical or project based and more focused on behavioral sciences, human resources, organizational development, or psychology (Kanter,

Stein, & Jick, 1992; Cummings & Worley, 2001; French & Bell, 1999; Caluwé & Vermaak, 2003). Attribution of failure of organizational change projects to poor management of human factors tends to add strength to this view (Buchanan & Boddy, 1992; By, 2005; Luo et al., 2006; Maguire & Redman, 2007).

While currently there is minimal cross-fertilization between publication by authors/researchers in the project management journals (*Project Management Journal* [PMJ], *International Journal of Project Management* [IJPM], *International Journal on Managing Projects in Business* [IJMPiB]) and the change management journals (e.g., the *Journal of Change Management* and the *Journal of Organizational Change Management*), one notable exception being Leybourne (2006, 2007), there is potential for a rich collaboration between the two fields. Project management tends to be considered practice rich and theory poor (Morris, 2002; Betts & Lansley, 1995), and change management has a rich theoretical foundation in organizational behavior and development (Cummings & Worley, 2001; Caluwé & Vermaak, 2003) but has experienced little by way of professional formation.

The research reported in this study sits at the intersection of change and project management and has therefore been informed by literature from both fields.

Scope of the Literature Review

As observed by Lehmann (2010, p. 328), the change management and project management fields contain many distinct conceptualizations and there is a huge gap between them as well as between the conceptualizations revealed over time, from the 1970s through to those developed in the 2000s. Bresnen (2006, pp. 73–74) sees the two fields as representing two different approaches to the "machinery of knowing" and says that is particularly noticeable in the way the project management field conceptualizes organization and management by drawing extensively upon operational research and systems theory applications and rather less perhaps upon behavioral and social theory. He refers to the organizational change and learning field as always having been significantly informed and shaped by work within the fields of organizational theory and behavior, psychology, sociology, and related disciplines.

Accordingly, the practices of project management and change implementation are clearly underpinned by different and distinct bodies of knowledge. Crawford and Hassner-Nahmias (2010, p. 406) also refer to the role of the change manager emerging from a different disciplinary background to that of the project manager. The latter they see as having its origins in engineering with a focus on planning and control, while organizational change as a discipline had grown from the organizational development field and places significant emphasis on the behavioral aspects of managing change. Lehmann (2010) likewise notes the tendency for project management practitioners to focus on planning, control, processes, and methodologies, while change implementation practitioners are more interested in "change's objects and underlying mechanisms" (p. 333) and the behavioral aspects of change.

Bresnen (2006, pp. 73–74) particularly saw the differences in the two epistemic cultures as being reflected in the way project management superimposes projects and their organizational settings on each other during the study of project management and organizational change processes. Most analyses in project management, in his view, naturally bring projects to the foreground, often depicting them as dynamic and set within a more or less static organizational context. This has tended to obscure understanding of how projects dovetail with the wider, changing lattice of organizational relationships in which they are embedded. Conversely, the organizational change and learning literature naturally brings the organizational context to the fore. Gareis and Huemann (2010, p. 311) noted a misperception in the project management community about the relationship between changes and programs (and projects). They refer to perceptions of change as being managed within programs (and projects) instead of perceiving programs (and projects) as organizations to manage the changes.

In accordance with the aims of the research reported in this paper, the literature review covers both the project management perspective on change and the change and general management perspective on project management. Examination of the full scope of organizational change research literature is outside the scope of this study. The span of the topics in the literature that have informed this study is presented in Figure 2-1.

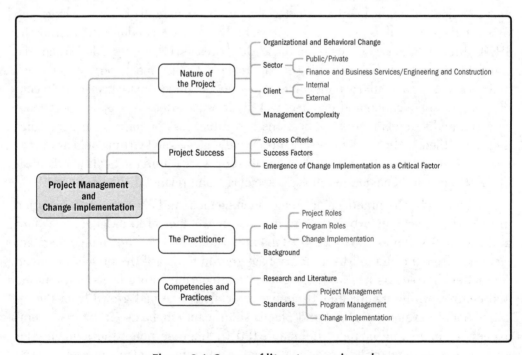

Figure 2-1. Scope of literature reviewed

This review includes the seminal resource and reference tool developed to help health care professionals in the United Kingdom National Health Service (NHS) find their way around the vast literature on change implementation and consider the evidence available concerning effectiveness of different approaches to change (Iles & Sutherland, 2001). This resource emerged from a national listening exercise carried out by the NHS to seek answers to questions about service delivery: why there was so often a gap between research evidence and implementation at the local level and what could be done to promote research as a lever for change.

The guide by Iles and Sutherland (2001) provides an accessible overview of change implementation approaches, including project management, as discerned from an NHS perspective. It describes approaches and concepts developed in schools of management, psychology, sociology, economics, and other fields during the preceding 50 years. Also, it discusses the context in which these approaches and concepts were developed, their potential use in the process of managing change, and the evidence available about their efficacy.

General problems identified with gathering and reviewing this evidence (Iles & Sutherland, 2001, p. 13) included these:

- For all but the simplest changes, the impact is multi-dimensional, which must be addressed in measures of effectiveness.
- Implementing and evaluating change programs is often an iterative process.
- Different people involved in a change program will have different views of the precipitating event or the underlying causes of the problem and desirable outcomes.

These problems highlight the challenges that management of multi-dimensional, multi-perspective, and iterative change may present to those who maintain a traditional, rational-linear view of project management.

The focus of this study, as expressed in the research questions, is on the importance of change facilitation knowledge and skills in the repertoire of project and program managers with a view to providing practical results for use by professional associations and practitioners. The literature for review has been selected accordingly. Not specifically addressed are particular mechanisms being adopted in organizations to promote/facilitate/manage change, including the project office (Morris, Patel, & Wearne, 2000; Huemann, Turner, & Keegan, 2004; Hobbs, Aubry, & Thuillier, 2008; Aubry, Müller, Hobbs, & Blomquist, 2010; Artto, Kulvik, Poskela, & Turkulainen, 2011), or research focused particularly on the process or content of organizational change.

Previous research drawing on the project and change implementation literatures and case studies of the relative roles and contributions of project/program managers and change managers in the implementation of organizational change indicated that project and program managers do not necessarily have the required competence to perform the full activities required to promote and implement the changes that they are leading as part of their projects (Crawford & Hassner-Nahmias, 2010, pp. 410–411). This is consistent with Iles and Sutherland's (2001, p. 70) finding that there is little explicit research evidence on the effectiveness of project management as a means to secure organizational change.

Nevertheless, in their framework, which clustered change management approaches around a small number of key questions, Iles and Sutherland (2001, p. 23) included project management along with organizational development, organizational learning/the learning organization, and action research under *how can we make change happen?*

The Nature of the Project and Its Management

The field of project management claims that projects bring about change and project management is recognized as the most efficient way of managing such change (APM, 2006, p. 2). In the *Glossary of Project Management Terms*, the APM acknowledges that the term "change management" may also be used to refer to a process whereby organizational change is introduced.

The primary standards for project management, however, provide little guidance on how to go about effecting desirable change that may involve dealing with organizational structure, culture, history, and politics (Pettigrew, McKee, & Ferlie, 1992). As Buchanan (1991) observed, "conventional project management texts and guides are typically based on the concept of the implementation life cycle" with a related expectation that the critical competencies of the project manager will be concerned with "project control, technical expertise, and communications" (p. 122). Twenty years later, as may generally be determined from the project management literature, this observation remains valid, although the success of many projects is understood to be dependent not only on the control of change, but on the proactive introduction of change, in varying degrees.

Within the project management literature there has been considerable criticism of the rational-linear view (Engwall, 2003; Cicmil et al., 2006) which is "increasingly seen by both researchers and organizational members enacting 'project management' in their daily practice, as inadequately addressing the complexity of projects in a theoretically sound and practically relevant way" (Cicmil, Cooke-Davies, Crawford, & Richardson, 2009, p. 2).

There are indications from the literature (Gareis & Huemann, 2010; Crawford & Hassner-Nahmias, 2010) that extension of primary standards for project management to include guidance for conduct of activities relating to the process and context of change could increase their relevance for project practitioners engaged in change implementation. This is becoming particularly challenging in a fast-moving global environment where many of the accepted rules of business no longer apply and where it is important for an organization to be able to renew its capabilities for change accordingly (Teece, Pisano, & Shuen, 1997; Teece, 2009).

This need for corporate change and renewal capability, promoted in the strategic management literature (Penrose, 1959; Teece et al., 1997), connects with attempts being made over the past decade in the project management literature to raise the strategic relevance of project management (Shenhar, 2004; Morris & Jamieson, 2005; Milosevic & Srivannaboon, 2006; Srivannaboon & Milosevic, 2006; Jugdev, Mathur, & Fung, 2007; Cooke-Davies, Crawford, & Lechler, 2009) and to reconnect project management to the broader management field. Leybourne (2007, p. 61) reports evidence that project-based research is moving from the tools and techniques of project management to a more behavioral bias, linking with some of the more established academic areas. This changing bias is arguably driven by organizational interest in flexible working, an encouragement of the channeling of creativity and innovation to create organizations that can survive and prosper in turbulent environments, and the dismantling of organizational bureaucracies, leading to a higher level of self-directed work activity.

Another important development has been the extension of interest beyond the limits of the stand-alone project, enriching the understanding of project management to include program (Pellegrinelli, 1997; Partington, Young, & Pellegrinelli, 2003; Lycett, Rassau, & Danson, 2004; Maylor, Brady, Cooke-Davies, & Hodgson, 2006; Artto, Martinsuo, Gemünden, & Murtoaro, 2009; Dietrich & Lehtonen, 2005) and portfolio management (Blomquist & Müller, 2006; Martinsuo & Lehtonen, 2007; Blichfeldt & Eskerod, 2008) and the recognition of project management as an organizational capability (Crawford, 2006; Aubry, Hobbs, & Thuillier, 2007, 2008; Hobbs et al., 2008; Jugdev et al., 2007; Aubry & Hobbs, 2011). Associated with these developments has been increasing interest in the relevance of context to the management of projects (Pellegrinelli, 2002; Engwall, 2003; Thomas & Mullaly, 2008).

There are many aspects of context that might be considered. Thomas and Mullaly (2005, 2008), with a team of 48 researchers, examined a wide range of contextual variables including those internal to the organization (such as strategic drivers, organizational culture, training, industry, project type, public versus private sector, size of organization, and experience of project professionals) and external to the organization (such as economic and political structure, funding sources for projects, and culture). Cooke-Davies et al. (2009) and Crawford and Cooke-Davies (2012) focused on the influence of strategic drivers as a contextual factor influencing the management of projects across a range of industry sectors. Besner and Hobbs (2011) also considered variations in practices across industry sectors and project types. They considered degree of complexity and innovation, level of project definition, and similarity to other projects as contextual variations. In previous work, they had also considered differences associated with projects undertaken for clients either internal or external to the performing organization (2008a).

In keeping with these and other studies, industry sector, nature of the client, and managerial complexity were considered in this research and will be briefly addressed in the literature review.

As we are considering the practices that need to be applied to management of organizational change projects as well as projects that require changes in either or both organizational structure and behavior in order to deliver desired outcomes, the degree of organizational and behavioral change is clearly a factor that needs to be addressed. Although the focus of this research is not specifically on theories of organizational change or "change's objects and underlying mechanisms" (Lehmann, 2010, p. 333), a general review of past and current practice provides context to the study.

Organizational and Behavioral Change

By (2005, p. 360, as cited in Moran & Brightman, 2001, p. 111) defines change management as the process of continually renewing an organization's direction, structure, and capabilities to serve the ever-changing needs of external and internal customers. However, as found by Ashurst and Hodges (2010) in their review of change management literature, there is no widely accepted, clear, and practical approach explaining what changes organizations need to make and how to implement them. By (2005, p. 320) reached a similar conclusion, finding it was difficult to identify any consensus regarding a framework for organizational change management. Further, the theories and approaches were often contradictory, mostly lacking empirical evidence, and supported by unchallenged hypotheses concerning the nature of contemporary organizational change management. Biedenbach and Söderholm (2008, p. 130) likewise refer to the basic lack of a valid framework for successful change implementation and to the need for more empirical evidence to overcome contradictions and confusions among theories and approaches within contemporary change management.

It is clear from the diversity of thinking and activity encompassed by the term "change," and the many change management approaches, models, and tools that may be extracted from the literature of many fields including project management (Iles & Sutherland, 2001, p. 14), that change is an ever-present feature of organizational life, both at an operational and strategic level. As reported in the literature, however, up to 70 percent of change initiatives fail (Higgs & Rowland, 2005, p. 122). Similarly, Iles and Sutherland (2001, p. 52) report a failure rate of between 50 percent to 70 percent of business process re-engineering initiatives to meet their cost, time, or productivity objectives.

Figure 2-2 presents the three different perspectives that Iles and Sutherland (2001) begin with to help focus thinking about the nature and scope of change. Given the diversity of change approaches identified in the change management literature, beginning with the perspectives represented in Table 2-1 appears as valid as any other approach in the literature reviewed. In this field, however, By (2005) refers

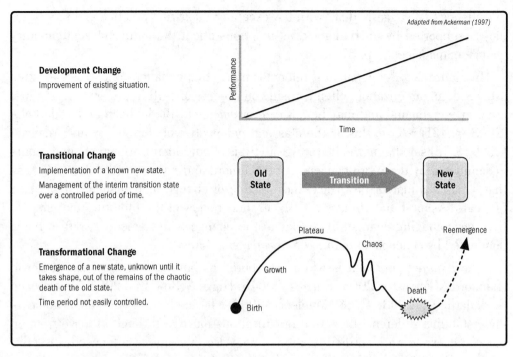

Figure 2-2. Perspectives on organizational change (Iles & Sutherland, 2001, p. 16)

Table 2-1. Planned and emergent change management approaches compared
(Biedenbach & Söderholm, 2008, pp. 133–134)

	Planned Change	Emergent Change
Characteristics	Top-down Coercive Elaborate plan for change Change as analytical rational process One best way of change for all organizations	Bottom-up Cooperative and organization-wide shared responsibility for change Organizations as open and fluid systems Power and politics as crucial aspects for change
Assumptions	Stable, predictable environment Identification of change need possible Change moves from a stable start position to a stable end through clear steps Employees are willing to change	Unpredictable, dynamic, and turbulent environment Change as a continuous process of adaptation and transformation to a rapidly changing environment All employees share responsibility for organizational change
Project linkage	Rational project selection	Bottom-up creation of change projects

to evidence that suggests that "with few exceptions, existing practice and theory are mostly supported by unchallenged assumptions about the nature of contemporary change management" (p. 370).

In Figure 2-2, *developmental* refers to change that enhances or corrects existing aspects of an organization, often focusing on process or skill improvement. It is first order or incremental and may be *planned* or *emergent*. Biedenbach and Söderholm (2008, p. 131) refer to this as the classical perspective of change. By and Macleod (2009, p. 13) say that in the literature, analysis of how organizational change occurs is dominated by these two concepts, and Bamford and Forrester (2003, p. 547) say that it has dominated the theory and practice of change management for the past 50 years. Ashurst and Hodges (2010), in their review of the literature on perspectives on managing change, also refer to the change management literature being dominated by concepts of *planned* and *emergent* change.

The *planned* approach is widely attributed as building on the work of Lewin (Bamford & Forrester, 2003; Burnes, 2004b; Higgs & Rowland, 2005; Biedenbach & Söderholm, 2008; By & Macleod, 2009). It emphasizes the importance of understanding different states that organizations must go through to move from an unsatisfactory to an identified desired state. Also, it requires a focused, directive manner. By (2005, p. 374) refers to the planned approach being long established and held to be highly effective, although subject to increasing criticism. Biedenbach and Söderholm (2008, p. 131), Bamford and Forrester (2003), and By (2005) also refer to criticism of the *planned* approach because it assumes organizations face stable conditions whereas organizations are increasingly facing dynamic and uncertain business environments (Brown & Eisenhardt, 1997; By, 2005; Higgs & Rowland, 2005; Self, Armenakis, & Schraeder, 2007; Ashurst & Hodges, 2010). Further, as observed by By (2005, p. 374), the *planned* approach presumes all stakeholders in a change management project are willing and interested in implementing it and that common agreement can be reached, a presumption that ignores organizational politics and conflict.

According to Iles and Sutherland (2001), arguably the central message of more recent change management literature is that "organizational-level change is not fixed or linear in nature but contains an important emergent element" (p. 14). By (2005, p. 375) says that the *emergent* approach should be perceived as a continuous open-ended process of adaptation to changing circumstances and conditions.

Bamford and Forrester (2003, p. 547) refer to the *emergent* change management approach as a relatively new concept that lacks the formal history of the *planned* approach. In their view, the *emergent* approach is "in theory, able to achieve a broader understanding of the problems of managing change within complex environments" (p. 548). They note the advocates of *emergent* change coming from a wide variety of backgrounds, each offering a distinctive view on how organizations should or should not manage change Nevertheless, By (2005) notes that being relatively new, the *emergent* approach can be viewed as lacking coherence and a diversity of techniques and "it consists of a rather disparate group of models and approaches that tend to be more united in their skepticism to the planned approach to change than to an agreed alternative" (p. 375).

Table 2-1 lists the comparative attributes of *planned* and *emergent* approaches as summarized by Biedenbach and Söderholm (2008).

Biedenbach and Soderholm (2008) considered neither approach suitable for the rapid and radical structural change occurring in their context and, accordingly, included additional change management approaches. The first, the "contingency approach" for change, citing Dunphy and Stace (1993), involved matching change approaches to an optimum fit with the changing environment and provided one best way of change for each organization. Under this approach, the change project would be aligned with environmental/organizational variables. The second approach, the "choice of change," aimed to achieve the benefits of a combined utilization of planned and emergent change. Burnes (2004a, p. 887) developed this approach in response to the idea that planned and emergent are competing approaches. He argued that, although Lewin's approach had often been portrayed by its critics as a simplistic approach to change, in fact it contained complex elements that Burnes (2004b) identified as field theory, group dynamics, and action research. In Biedenbach and Söderholm's summary (2008, pp. 133–134), the project linkage for this approach is a situation-dependent choice of change project.

While noting that there are no universal rules when it comes to leading and managing change, By (2005, p. 375) refers to several advocates of the emergent approach who have suggested sequences of actions that organizations could comply with. However, citing Burnes (2004c), he notes that many of these tend to be abstract and difficult to apply. He then refers to authors offering practical guidance for organizations and managers, including Kanter et al.'s (1992) "Ten Commandments for Executive Change" and Kotter's (1996) "Eight-Stage Process for Organisational Transformation." In their examination of organizational change philosophies and their underpinning assumptions, Graetz and Smith (2011) refer to these approaches, along with Hammer and Champy's (1993) "business process re-engineering," as offering a formulaic approach that presupposes that organizational change can and should be a controlled and orderly affair. Quinn (1996, 2004) and Cameron and Quinn (2005) offer a less formulaic and more values focus and emergent approach that focuses on the role of the change leader and the processes involved in changing organizational culture.

The term "transitional," given by Iles and Sutherland (2001) to the second change mode represented in Figure 2-2, refers to change that seeks to achieve a known, desired state that is different from the existing one. It is episodic, planned, and radical (second order). Iles and Sutherland (2001, p. 15) say this model is the basis of much of the organizational change literature. They attribute its foundations to the work of Lewin (1951) who conceptualized the process as involving unfreezing the existing organizational equilibrium, moving to a new position, and refreezing to the new equilibrium position. The third change mode, transformational, refers to radical or second order change, which requires a shift in assumptions made by the organization (Iles & Sutherland, 2001, p. 16). Therefore, it may "result in the creation of an organisation that operates in development mode – one that continuously learns, adapts and improves" (p.16). By (2005, p. 377) refers to transformational change being identified by major shifts of departments/divisions within an organization that may be radical.

Another distinction Iles and Sutherland make (2001, pp. 14–15), as cited in Weick and Quinn (1999), is episodic (second order), or discontinuous, versus continuous (first order) change. Weick and Quinn (1999) had made the distinction based on differences in analytic frameworks, ideal organizations, intervention theories, roles for agents, and implied metaphors of organizing. Under episodic change, organizations are inertial and change is infrequent, discontinuous, and intentional, while under the continuous change mode, organizations are self-organizing and change is constant, evolving, and cumulative (Weick & Quinn, 1999, p. 365).

Ashurst and Hodges (2010, pp. 219–220) distinguish between the punctuated equilibrium model of change, which assumes organizations accomplish transformations discontinuously, and the continuous transformation model, which seeks to apply complexity theories to organizational change (Brown & Eisenhardt, 1997). They suggest, citing Bamford and Forrester (2003), that it is the uncertainty of an organization's external and internal environment that makes the latter approach the more pertinent. By (2005) refers to an apparent consensus among contemporary authors that the benefits of discontinuous change do not last. A better approach is continuous change, whereby "organizations and their people continually monitor, sense and respond to the external and internal environment in small steps as an ongoing process" (p. 372); however, By (2005) notes it is not a smooth process. He suggests a five-fold classification of change characteristics: discontinuous, incremental, bumpy incremental, continuous, and bumpy continuous.

As represented by Iles and Sutherland (2001), however, it is the concept of transitional change that arguably more closely aligns than the other two with the current, rational-linear view of a project predominant in the project management standards, wherein, as Gareis observes (2010, p. 316), "the term 'change' is related only to a 'change in scope' due to a change order by a client."

An example of a recent endeavor to start bridging the gap between change management and project management is provided in a special issue of the *International Journal of Project Management* (Gareis & Huemann, 2010, p. 311). Figure 2-3 is Gareis' (2010, p. 321) categorization of types of change applying to permanent

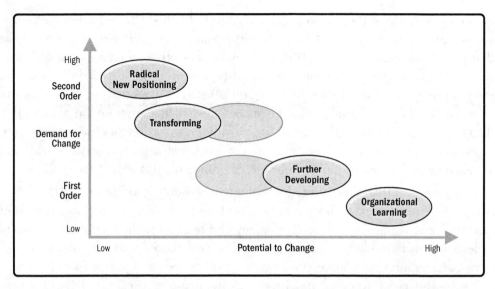

Figure 2-3. Definition of change types according to hypotheses formulated from a combination of action research and conventional social research based on case studies from different organizations (Gareis, 2010, p. 318)

organizations according to the demand for change, distinguishing between first order and second order changes, and potential for change, which is defined as the availability of individual and organizational competencies for managing the respective changes. In another paper, Eskerod (2010, p. 353) refers to the importance of differentiating between these various types of changes in order to better grasp the challenges related to each of these specific change types and to define appropriate and relevant processes, activities, and roles. In the special issue papers, the predominant concepts of change elaborated are Gareis' (2010) transforming change models (Gareis, 2010; Huemann, 2010; Fiedler, 2010; Stummer & Zuchi, 2010; Cowan-Sahadath, 2010) and further developing change models (Beldi, Cheffi, & Dey, 2010; Eskerod, 2010), which may be seen as related to the emergent and continuous (and non-radical) transformation referred to earlier (Brown & Eisenhardt, 1997; Weick & Quinn, 1999).

During transformation, the strategies, structures, and cultures of an organization, as well as its relationships to relevant environments, are changed (Gareis, 2010, p. 321). Lehmann (2010, p. 330) refers to transforming changes as second-order changes that involve a paradigmatic shift. These are distinguished from the conventional conception of mostly first order change management, which will not review the underlying organizational assumptions and values.

Gareis (2010) sees the challenges of transforming change to be in the managing of contradiction. In this respect, it is similar to his category of radical new-positioning, the highest demand/lowest potential to change on his scale, wherein one has to deal with high social complexity, the uniqueness of the situation, time pressure, and high dynamics because of the ongoing daily business. In this categorization, organizational learning is represented as having the lowest demand/highest potential for change. As defined by Gareis (2010, p. 320), the objectives of organizational learning are the assurance of a continuous quality improvement in the daily business and the promotion of innovation in an organization. The objectives of the remaining category, "further developing," which is represented as first order on the "demand for change" axis, are to maintain and/or improve the business results by implementing major improvements and innovations in products, markets, the organization, the infrastructure, or relationships to relevant environments (Gareis, 2010, p. 321).

Huemann's (2010) case study found human resource management (HRM) services, processes, and organization to be a central dimension of transformation from a hierarchical to a project-oriented company and referred to the challenges faced by project managers, including concerns relating to authority and responsibility; careers, salaries, and promotion; employee wellbeing; and stress. An earlier literature review by Huemann, Keegan, and Turner (2007) found most extant HRM literature was essentially framed in terms of large, stable organizations and HRM in flat and flexible project-oriented companies had generally been neglected. They referred to this as a missing link between the project management (PM) and HRM literature. From her later study, Huemann (2010, p.368) concluded that project management competencies raise the potential for transforming a company, and on the other hand the demand for transforming supports the professionalization of project management.

Huemann (2010) refers to specific competencies and capabilities of project-oriented companies being described in literature, including by Söderlund and Tell (2009), who extended previous reported findings on firm-level capabilities by integrating analyses of project competence. Söderlund and Tell (2009, p. 102) considered organizational capabilities within the context of the knowledge-based theory of the firm, whereby the firm is seen as an institution for integrating knowledge. They argued that the evolutionary analysis approach suggested in their paper would improve understanding of the emergence and evolution of a firm's dynamic capabilities.

The concept of dynamic capabilities has been a developing area in general change management literature (Teece, Pisano, & Shuen, 1997, as cited in Pandza & Thorpe, 2009). Pandza and Thorpe (2009, p. S119) argue that dynamic capability in a particular firm is demonstrated if the firm is creating novel knowledge that is not determined by the experiential dynamics of existent knowledge trajectories. Zahra, Sapienza, and Davidsson (2006, p. 918) distinguish dynamic capabilities, defined as abilities to reconfigure a firm's resources and routines in the manner envisioned and deemed appropriate by its principal decision makers, from substantive capabilities. Substantive capability, in their view, is the ability to solve a problem. Therefore, a new routine for product development would be a new substantive capability, while the ability to change such capabilities is a dynamic capability. They refer to the literature in the field as being "in its infancy" and to confusion and lack of agreement on the nature of dynamic capabilities and to the emergent discussion of dynamic capabilities in the (change management) literature being grounded in the evolutionary theory of the firm.

Building on the emergent literature, Zahra et al. (2006, p. 920) present a stylized model of the various activities associated with the creation of dynamic capabilities and how they may relate to each other (Figure 2-4). As implied by this model, over time the recombining of substantive capabilities increases the firm's ability to conceive and implement varied, multiple, and innovative strategic responses to its environmental challenges.

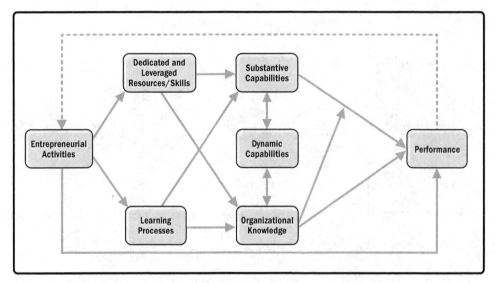

Figure 2-4. A stylized model of capability formation and performance (Zahra, Sapienza, & Davidsson 2006, p. 920)

Reviewing the findings from recent literature, Ashurst and Hodges (2010) say that the focus on dynamic capabilities "shifts the emphasis from succeeding with a specific change or transformation initiative to the wider issue of the 'benefits realization capability' of the organization: the ability to select the right change initiatives; to approach them in the right way; to successfully deliver them; and then to sustain and exploit the results" (pp. 221–222). In their view, dynamic capability requires a range of individuals with different knowledge and skills working together in multi-disciplinary, cross-functional teams. Further, to be effective, a common language, some level of common experience, and common process is needed (Eskerod & Riis, 2009). Routines ("practices") representing the work people do can be the basis for establishing a common approach, or a specific way of working, as part of a substantive or dynamic organizational capability. These practices can be shared within or between organizations.

From their research, Ashurst and Hodges (2010) found a number of themes related to the nature of organizational competence emerging that were not adequately reflected in the descriptions from their literature review. Therefore, they established a revised perspective on how competence can be conceptualized within the "black box" of an organization (Figure 2-5). This includes three aspects of competencies, as they may contribute to the overall benefits realization capability, not identified in previous work (Peppard & Ward, 2004): paradigm (or principles); relationships (a crucial element of the required competences); and practices (routines).

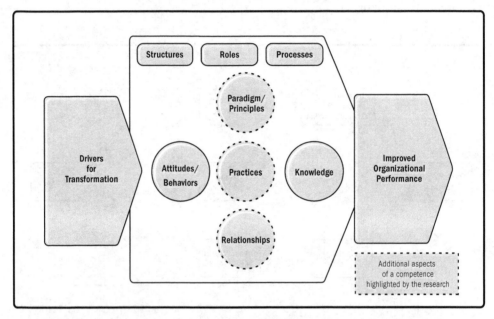

Figure 2-5. A model of competences for benefits realization within the "black box" of the formal organization that extends major perspectives reported in the literature (Ashurst & Hodges, 2010, p. 234)

Ashurst and Hodges (2010, p. 231) reported that many of the participants in their research emphasized the importance of individual skills and experience in the success of benefits realization initiatives. In response to recognition of skill gaps, some participants were attending or aiming to attend project management education (including PRINCE2 and *Managing Successful Programmes*), while others were being supported by ongoing coaching and support. This work confirms a nexus between change implementation, project management, and the realization of benefits.

Industry Sector

Review of the various approaches to organizational change, as covered in the previous section, highlights the pervasiveness of change implementation across all industry sectors. This is not surprising, as organizations must increasingly respond to environmental change, including "new government regulations, new products, growth, increased competition, technological developments, and a changing workforce" (Kotter & Schlesinger, 2008, p. 130). Some of these responses may be considered organizational changes, but others may be conceptualized in other ways, and many, but not all, may be conceived and treated as projects. In business and commerce, projects represent a substantial proportion of the productive effort of enterprises in every industrial sector. The range of products that are created or modified by projects gives some indication of the extent and value of project work to industry, and of the beneficial change that projects achieve:

- New facilities are produced—factories, offices, plants, or pieces of infrastructure. These are then operated for economic advantage.
- New products are designed or developed for manufacture in ongoing operations or for use to generate wealth in some other way.
- Services are delivered, such as the refit of a ship, the renovation of a building or the conduct of a piece of research.
- Changes are engineered to business systems and to organization structures so that enterprises can be operated more efficiently.

Indeed, project management and project modes of organizing are becoming central to industrial competitiveness (Davies & Hobday, 2005; Morris & Pinto, 2004; Pinto, 2006; Flyvbjerg, Bruzelius, & Rothengatter, 2003; Miller & Lessard, 2001). Although both change and projects are prevalent across all industry sectors, a number of studies (Pinto & Covin, 1989; Cooke-Davies & Arzymanow, 2003; Crawford & Pollack, 2007; Besner & Hobbs, 2008; Thomas & Mullaly, 2008; Crawford & Cooke-Davies, 2012) have demonstrated variations in use of practices in management of different types of projects and in different markets or industries such as engineering and construction, information technology, pharmaceutical R & D, defense, and financial services. Numerous studies investigating particular project types confirm the importance of distinguishing between different types of projects and different industries suggesting that, in considering the relationship between project management and change implementation, there would be value in investigating the possibility of differences in use of practices across industry sectors.

Public or private sector context may also be expected to exert some influence on use of project management and change implementation practices. The government sector is a specific context with distinctive characteristics that may have a different impact from the private sector on use of project, program, and change practices and practitioner role. As observed by Crawford and Helm (2009), the importance of project and program management capability in the public sector has been recognized in government initiatives in various countries in most cases associated with increasing public scrutiny and a need for assurance of value from public expenditure. The

U.S. government has invested significantly in project and program management, notably in Defense Acquisition, the Department of Energy, and NASA (NASA, 2008). In the United Kingdom, the Office of Government Commerce (OGC) was established to "help Government deliver best value from its spending," including the "delivery of projects to time, quality and cost, realizing benefits" (Office of Government Commerce, 2008). The OGC, which ceased to exist because of the change of U.K. government in 2010, worked with public sector organizations to help them improve their efficiency, gain better value for money from their commercial activities, and deliver improved success from programs and projects. They provided considerable support for management of projects and programs, including well-known and widely used methodologies and guides such as PRINCE2 (Office of Government Commerce, 2009) and *Managing Successful Programmes* (Office of Government Commerce, 2007; U.K. Cabinet Office, 2011). Management of organizational change, particularly through programs, has been a dominant theme throughout these initiatives of the U.K. government. Review of the literature, including the work of Iles and Sutherland (2001) referenced in the previous section, demonstrates the high level of interest in organizational change and organizational change projects in the public sector. This may in part be attributable to the recurring need to respond to changes of government (Riddell & Haddon, 2009). There is certainly sufficient evidence to suggest that investigation of differences between public and private sector practices may be fruitful.

Nature of the Client

Most recently, Besner and Hobbs (2008) identified differences in use of practices on projects delivered to customers internal to the organization as opposed those delivered to external customers. They concluded that the traditional project management toolkit is primarily suited to large, well-defined projects for clients external to the performing organization and that there was a need to adapt project management practices to suit less well defined projects delivered to internal clients. Cost/benefit analysis was the only tool they found that was being used more on projects for internal rather than external clients.

Where organizational change is the primary focus it is reasonable to assume that the clients are more likely to be internal rather than external, suggesting that the nature of the client may be an influencing factor in the use of project management and change implementation practices.

Managerial Complexity

When considering the nature of projects, and how this might influence the practices that are applied in managing them, one of the attributes most commonly used by organizations is complexity (Crawford, Hobbs, & Turner, 2006). Complexity is not, however, a single construct but a composite attribute that draws upon a variety of constituent characteristics. Attributes commonly used in practice to signify complexity include project scope, risk, technical difficulty, and number of functions or skills involved (Crawford, Hobbs, & Turner, 2005). A distinction may also be made between the complexity of the project and the complexity of its management.

Much has been written about the complexity of projects and their management (Baccarini, 1996; Williams, 2002; Geraldi, 2008; Cooke-Davies, Cicmil, Crawford, & Richardson, 2007; Cicmil et al., 2009; Remington & Pollack, 2007; Remington, 2011; Cooke-Davies, Crawford, Patton, Stevens, & Williams, 2011), giving rise to a number of different but related characterizations. For instance, Shenhar and Dvir (1996) proposed a model comprising four levels of technological uncertainty and three levels of system scope. Drawing upon the work of Turner and Cochrane (1993) and Williams (2002), Remington and Pollack (2007) provided another useful categorization of project related complexity:

- Structural complexity: involving multiple interconnected tasks and activities;
- Technical complexity: involving novelty and multiple interdependent solution options;
- Directional complexity: involving ambiguity arising from multiple interpretations of goals and objectives; and
- Temporal complexity: involving uncertainty due to shifting environmental and strategic directions.

Bosch-Rekveldt (2011, pp. 82–83) conducted an extensive review of the literature and identified forty elements contributing to project complexity. From this and from analysis of case studies and interviews, she developed the TOE complexity framework that addresses technical, organizational, and external complexity (p. 213) (see also Bosch-Rekveldt, Jongkind, Mooi, Bakker, & Verbraeck, 2011).

In practice, the Australian Defence Materiel Organisation uses six attributes—three dimensions of cost (requirements development cost, acquisition cost, and whole of life cost), technical difficulty, nature of operation and support infrastructure, and commercial aspects—as a basis for categorizing their projects and programs and determining their management (Defence Materiel Organisation, 2004).

The Global Alliance for Project Performance Standards (GAPPS) has devised a seven-factor model for assessing the management complexity of projects (GAPPS, 2007). These seven factors can be summarized as follows: strategic importance; number of organizational interfaces; stakeholder cohesion; number of disciplines and methods; financial impact; stability of context; and legal, social, and environmental implications. Although assessment against these dimensions is both subjective and relative, research and practice indicate a high level of agreement between assessments made by managers of projects, by independent assessors, and by senior managers (Aitken & Crawford, 2007).

Regardless of these various frameworks for categorizing the complexity of projects and their management, a distinguishing factor between what is complicated and complex appears to be the involvement of people (Cooke-Davies et al., 2011, p. ix). It is therefore reasonable to assume that degree of organizational and behavioral change can be considered indicative of level of and associated with increasing levels of managerial complexity.

Project Success

Project success has been a popular topic in the project management literature, as reviews and summaries of the subject show (e.g., Kloppenborg & Opfer, 2000; Cooke-Davies, 2004; Jugdev & Müller, 2005; Ika, 2009). Critical success factors (CSFs) that have been investigated have included those related to the project, to the project manager and team, to the organization, and to the external environment (Belassi & Tukel, 1996; Jugdev & Müller, 2005). The majority of this research, although acknowledging that certain external factors such as the need for top management support are important, has been project-centric. It has focused on the implementation phase and, in line with the traditional view of projects as phenomena isolated from their context (Engwall, 2003), has primarily been examining factors internal to the project that can be seen as having a favorable, or unfavorable, influence on performance.

Interest in factors contributing to the success of projects, often referred to as critical success factors, began in the 1960s (Cooke-Davies, 2002; Fortune & White, 2006). In the following 20 years, two major aspects of success came to be generally accepted, the first being how it is judged (success criteria) and the second being the factors that contribute to its achievement (success factors). Often the two are confused and the same phenomena may be used as either a criterion for judgment or a factor contributing to achievement of a desired outcome, or both.

Success Criteria

In terms of success criteria, there is now general agreement on a distinction between project management success, concerned with internal measures of project performance such as time, cost, and quality, and project success, measured against the overall objectives of the project (Belassi & Tukel, 1996; Cooke-Davies, 2002; Jugdev & Müller, 2005). Following considerable debate concerning the criteria by which both project management success and project success are judged, it has become generally accepted that success is an ambiguous concept that may be judged differently from different stakeholder perspectives (Lim & Mohamed, 1999; Piyush, Dangayach, & Mittal, 2011).

Although the inherent ambiguity of success has presented a challenge to researchers endeavoring to identify factors that contribute to its achievement, a review of research in the field reveals that most studies generally follow the definition provided by Baker, Murphy, and Fisher (1988), that project success is a matter of perception and that a project will be most likely to be perceived as an "overall success" if:

> . . . the project meets the technical performance specifications and/or mission to be performed, and if there is a high level of satisfaction concerning the project outcome among key people on the project team, and key users or clientele of the project effort. (p. 902)

Furthermore, there is general agreement that although time and budget performance alone are considered inadequate as measures of project success, they are still important components of the overall construct. Project management success can therefore be seen as a component of project success.

Patanakul, Iewwongcharoen, and Milosevic (2010, p. 45), in examining the literature on project success, proposed that dimensions for judging project success could be categorized into internal or project related criteria (time, cost, and performance), customer related criteria (satisfaction, actual utilization, and benefits), and organization related criteria (financial, market, and benefits). They further observed that these categories reflected the recognition of value creation as an important objective of project management (Winter, Anderson, Elvin, & Levene, 2006). By including benefits realization as a measure of success, these categories also recognize that project success may be extended to encompass the success of the product of the project.

Success Factors

The work of Murphy, Baker, and Fisher (1974), using a sample of 650 completed aerospace, construction, and other projects with data provided primarily by project managers, remains the most extensive and authoritative research on the factors contributing to project success. Their work has been cited and used in the majority of subsequent research papers on the subject. Ten factors were found to have a strong linear relationship to both perceived success and perceived failure of projects, while 23 project management characteristics were identified as being necessary but not sufficient conditions for perceived success (Baker et al., 1988).

Important work was conducted on project success factors in the 1980s, notably by Pinto and Slevin (1987, 1988) and Morris and Hough (1993). Both studies draw on the research of Murphy et al. (1974) and have been regularly cited in later work. While Morris and Hough (1993) drew primarily on literature and case study analysis of major projects, Pinto and Slevin (1987, 1988) based their findings on the opinions of a usable sample of 418 PMI members responding to questions asking them to rate the relevance to project implementation success of 10 critical success factors (Slevin & Pinto, 1986) and four additional external factors.

Further studies aimed at identifying factors contributing to the success, and in some cases, the failure, of projects (Ashley, Lurie, & Jaselskis, 1987; Geddes, 1990; Clarke, 1995; Clarke, 1999; Lechler, 1998; Jiang, Klein, & Balloun, 1996; Zimmerer & Yasin, 1998) used methodologies similar to that of Pinto and Slevin, with findings based on ratings, or in some cases, rankings, of success factors by project personnel, general managers, or other professionals. Beale and Freeman (1991) identified 14 variables that affect achievement of project success from a review of 29 papers. Wateridge (1996) identified eight most often mentioned success factors from a review of literature reporting results of empirical research relating to IS/IT projects. Lechler (1998), drawing on a large sample survey and strong statistical methods, established the importance of the human factors in project success. Cooke-Davies (2001, 2002) drew upon empirical research from more than 70 large multi-national or national organizations to identify 12 factors critical to project success.

Three papers are particularly useful in providing an understanding of research and scholarship relating to critical success factors for projects. Jugdev and Müller (2005) reviewed the evolution of understanding of project success over the preceding 40 years, summarizing views on both success criteria and factors. Fortune and White (2006) reviewed 63 publications that focus on critical success factors and present a synthesis and summary of the success factors listed in descending order of frequency of occurrence. They note that the three most cited factors are: the importance of senior management support, clear and realistic objectives, and production of an efficient plan. Ika (2009) provides a further review of both project success criteria and factors. Although this review is limited to articles published in project management journals between 1986 and 2004, its contribution goes beyond the actual criteria and factors identified, taking a more philosophical view and identifying a trend from an initial focus on different aspects of control (Westerveld, 2003) towards a more contextually and socially embedded understanding of project success.

Research into factors that contribute to the success of projects, subsequent to and therefore not covered by the reviews by Jugdev and Müller (2005), Fortune and White (2006) and Ika (2009), represent a tension between studies that are focused on control within the project and those that attempt to address softer issues, both internal and external to the project, including context and human factors. Those researchers searching for critical success factors within the project have focused on the contribution of traditional project management tools, techniques, and practices to the success of projects. For instance, Besner and Hobbs (2006) drew upon practitioner perceptions of the relative value of different project management tools, techniques, and practices to identify those that have potential to contribute to the improved performance of projects. Patanakul et al. (2010) asked 412 project managers to rate how often they used 39 selected project management tools and techniques on a recently completed project. Zwikael and Globerson (2006) asked 282 project managers to rank the impact of 16 planning processes on project success, and Zwikael (2009) conducted a study involving 783 project managers from different countries and industries in order to identify the relative importance of the nine Knowledge Areas in the *PMBOK® Guide* (PMI, 2008a) during project planning in terms of contribution to project success. Any study will be limited by its focus and the questions that are asked of respondents. The studies that ask only about the use of traditional project management tools, techniques, and practices will only provide answers within this range.

Researchers who have looked beyond the use of tools, techniques, and practices of project management as represented in the most widely accepted standards (PMI, 2008a; IPMA, 2006; APM, 2006) have investigated the influence of organizational culture (Yazici, 2009; Belassi & Tukel, 1996; Belassi, Kondra, & Tukel, 2007); behavioral competencies of the project manager (Cheng & Dainty, 2005; Müller & Turner, 2007b; Thomas & Buckle-Henning, 2007; Aitken & Crawford, 2008; Thi & Swierczek, 2010); fit between the project manager and the project (Malach-Pines, Dvir, & Sadeh, 2009); leadership (Müller & Turner, 2007a; Anantatmula, 2010; Geoghegan & Dulewicz, 2008; Piyush et al., 2011); vision (Christensen & Walker, 2008); knowledge sharing (Ismail, Nor, & Marjani, 2009), and social embeddedness and cultural characteristics (Rai, Maruping, & Venkatesh, 2009).

Emergence of Change Implementation as a Critical Success Factor

Human dimensions and the implementation of change are significant emergent themes in recent studies of factors contributing to the success of projects. Nicholas and Hidding (2010) suggest that attempts to improve the success of information technology projects has been hampered by the focus on "variations of the traditional project management paradigm as promulgated" (p. 147) in standards and propose looking beyond traditional approaches to find other factors that might increase the likelihood of project success. Working with an expert panel, they developed a set of principles centered around value-driven change leadership, stating that "since change is inherent to projects, project managers should address issues related to successful change such as learning, consensual agreement, change support, and treating people as individuals" (Nicholas & Hidding, 2010, p. 150).

Levasseur (2010) suggests that use of "the most effective models, methods, and processes of organization development (OD), also known as change management" has potential to improve "the odds of project success" (p. 159). He further proposes that to improve the human side of project implementation, project managers should "learn how to apply some simple and elegant approaches to facilitating change from the change management expert's toolkit" (p. 160). Importance of change implementation as a factor contributing to the success of projects is confirmed by Tan et al. (2009) in the context of enterprise resource planning (ERP) projects, and by Martin (2011), who found a positive correlation between a well developed and implemented change management strategy and the success of shared service projects.

It is important to note, at this point, that although "effective change management" appears in the top third of critical success factors derived by Fortune and White (2006) from a review of 63 publications, they use the term not in the organizational development and behavior sense of processes for implementation of desirable change, but in the project management sense of effective control of (undesirable) change to the baselines of the project. Although project managers claim that projects "bring about change and project management is recognized as the most efficient way of managing such change" (APM, 2006, p. 2), Crawford et al. (Crawford & Hassner-Nahmias, 2010; Crawford, Aitken, & Hassner-Nahmias, 2011a) point out that the primary standards for project management provide little guidance concerning implementation of desirable change as described by Lavasseur (2010). Therefore, apart from a small number of recent studies, primarily relating to information studies, change implementation practices have not been included as candidates for identification as critical success factors for projects.

Emergence of change implementation as a factor contributing to the success of projects can be seen as associated with both treatment of an increasing range of initiatives as projects and the extension of understanding of project success to encompass value creation and the delivery of benefits. Even projects that are not specifically concerned with organizational change or renewal are likely to require some changes to structures, routines, or behaviors in order to ensure that the project creates value (Lechler & Byrne, 2010). In most cases, these changes will need to take place in the permanent organization that is the recipient of the product of the project. Effective transfer of the product of the project to the business, ensuring readiness of the business to accept and utilize the outputs of the project to ensure delivery of benefits, is therefore vital if the project is to achieve the purposes for which it was devised.

In summary, project success is now recognized as a multi-dimensional concept, subject to varying stakeholder perspectives. Criteria for judgment of success may include traditional measures of project management performance such as time, cost, and delivery to specification (quality), plus measures of customer satisfaction and organization related measures such as delivery of benefits. Research to identify factors critical to the success of projects has tended to be project-centric, aimed at identifying necessary conditions and tools, techniques and practices in the traditional project management toolkit that are most closely associated with project success. Extension of project success beyond the traditional project life cycle to include transfer to operations and delivery of benefits highlights the need to broaden the search for critical success factors. Realization of benefits and value creation require effective partnership between projects and operations and will often require changes to structures, routines, and behaviors. Recent research suggests that keys to success may be found beyond the project management toolkit, in associated fields such as organizational change management.

Role and Background of the Practitioner

Strummer and Zuchi (2010) claim that a clear definition of change roles and project/program roles is missing from both the change and project management literatures even though change is generally recognized to be of utmost importance in today's organizations.

In practice, change implementation may involve a number of different roles and an individual may carry out more than one of them. Change roles can be expected to include those with the title of change manager as well as those in human resource management, communications, and other related roles including that of business analyst, as associated with business process re-engineering.

In the project management field, change implementation is seen as involving people from both the permanent (operational) and temporary (project) parts of organizations (Turner & Müller, 2003). In keeping with Buchanan's (1991) identification of three different literatures concerned with change, the roles involved in change implementation can be similarly categorized in that there are those drawn from the project management community (e.g., project managers and team members), those involved in operations or general management (e.g., CEO, divisional and business unit managers with responsibilities for implementing change), and change implementation personnel who may be consultants or members of the human resource management function within the organization. Program managers, considered in the project management field as having a key role in organizational change projects, may be drawn from the project, business/general management, or change implementation communities.

Pellegrinelli et al. (2007) have pointed out that program and change managers need to focus on business and people issues rather than technical solutions, creating a strong team environment, communicating with confidence at all levels, and understanding the nature and difference of cultures and how they interact in organizations. This view is supported by Balogun and Hailey (2008), who claim that program managers need to develop analytical and judgmental skills as well as their sensitivity, self-awareness, and ability to handle complexity and deal with power issues in organizations. It is important to note that all of these skills are more concerned with process than control, the latter being the primary focus of those coming from a project management background (Buchanan, 1991). A role that has been identified as relevant in change related projects, primarily as a responsibility of program management (Crawford & Hassner-Nahmias, 2010; Office of Government Commerce [OGC], 2007) is benefits management.

Primary standards for project management (APM, IPMA, and PMI) suggest introduction of organizational change is the province of the program or line management rather than the project: "If the project concerns organizational change, then the change to be implemented as an outcome of the project is managed by line management, not by the project team" (IPMA, 2006, p. 16). The *PMBOK® Guide* (PMI, 2008a) states that change is something that the program manager, rather than the project manager, must expect and be prepared to manage.

Practices and Competencies

A study by Crawford and Hassner-Nahmias (2010) provides a project management perspective of the expected competencies of project, program, and change managers based on review of the project and change management literatures and case studies of the relative roles and contributions of project/program managers as change managers in the implementation of organizational change. They found that while there were apparent similarities in what was expected of people in project, program, and change roles, particularly in terms of communication, stakeholder relationships, and planning, there were significant qualitative differences in what they did in practice, as presented in Figure 2-6.

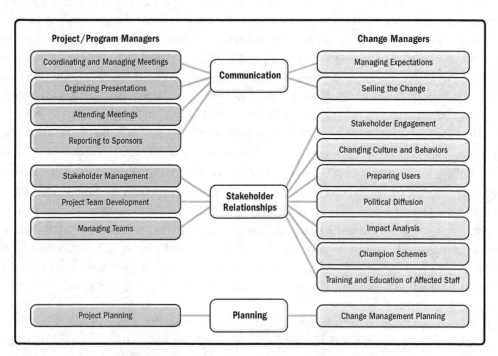

Figure 2-6. What project/program managers and change agents do (Crawford, Aitken, & Hassner-Nahmias, 2011b [based on results presented in Crawford & Hassner-Nahmias [2010])

Project and program managers, in communications and stakeholder relationships, are concerned with coordination, control, and management of the project, tending toward an internal focus on the project team and formal reporting arrangements. On the other hand, those with a primary role in change implementation are more concerned with the context of the project and the people who will be affected. They are more concerned with engagement rather than management of stakeholders, with management of expectations, promotion, and acceptance of the change including preparation of users such as training and education. While those in project, program, and change roles are all involved with planning, project and program managers are concerned with the planning of the project and those in change roles are primarily concerned with planning of the necessary changes.

The qualitative differences indicated in Figure 2-6 are consistent with Lehmann's (2010, p. 333) comparison of project management and change management approaches focusing on communication. As suggested by Lehmann (2010), project management communication is a tool for coordination and control ("traditional school") and also for building the project through collaboration ("renewal school"). For change management, it is a tool to convince and spread ("classical school") through dialogue and debates ("actual school").

The results reported in Crawford and Hassner-Nahmias (2010) may also be explained by the three agendas derived by Buchanan (1991) from an analysis of project management, general, and sociological literatures. He deduced that project managers will have a "control agenda," as represented in the project management standards, concerned with project planning, sequencing, budgeting, and monitoring. General management and those concerned with change implementation will have a "process agenda" focusing on managerial and organizational issues including communication, participation, negotiation, influence, team-building, and the management of meaning, symbols, values, and rituals. According to Buchanan, this process agenda is "not ignored by the conventional literature of project management, but is typically not emphasized, works with a rational-linear perspective of process and does not adequately express the importance of the political dimensions of organizational change" (p. 124).

The focus of the research by Crawford and Hassner-Nahmias (2010) was on performance-based competencies evidenced by what is done in the workplace, rather than personal competencies, while nevertheless observing that the change management literature strongly emphasizes the latter's importance for effective change management. Crawford and Hassner-Nahmias (2010, pp. 405–406) refer to the popular view in the project management community of project managers being managers of change or change agents (citing Turner et al., 1996). However, they also note that others, including Partington et al. (2005), consider that projects or programs that require significant amounts of behavioral and organizational change "demand high levels of interpersonal skill, astuteness and sensitivity and a fundamentally different approach to the candid, direct, and rational style valued in competent project managers. They need to learn skills and capabilities beyond those required to manage a typical project in order to drive change" (Crawford & Hassner-Nahmias, 2010, p. 406).

From their review, Crawford and Hassner-Nahmias (2010, p. 408) concluded that the change management literature makes it clear that organizational context is a major factor determining the approach to be taken and this will, in turn, influence the competencies required. As observed by Nieminen and Lehtonen (2008), in the dynamic and complex business environment of organizations today, the traditional functional and hierarchical organizing of work no longer offers best performance. In this new environment, according to Nikolaou, Gouras, Vakola, and Bourantis (2007, p. 291) it is important to be able to recruit and select people capable of bringing or initiating change as well as able to handle it effectively. There have been, however, few attempts to study the dispositional characteristics and competencies required by these "change agents."

Higgs and Rowland (2005) examine leadership behaviors in promoting organizational change. They refer to a stream of research that demonstrates clear linkages between leader behaviors and a variety of "follower" behaviors and performance measures; however, this research fails to link directly with the change literature (p. 126). Studies that have responded to the challenge of providing insights into the actual behavior of leaders have tended to conclude that "for effective leadership there are a relatively small number of broad areas of behaviour which are executed in somewhat differentiated ways depending on the personality of the leader" (p. 127). They noted few studies moved beyond generic descriptions, with the exceptions reported in Higgs and Rowland (2000) where leadership behaviors were specifically linked to activities involved in implementing change. They identified five broad areas of leadership competency associated with successful change implementation:

1. Creating the case for change: effectively engaging others in recognizing the business need for change.
2. Creating structural change: ensuring that the change is based on depth of understanding of the issues and supported with a consistent set of tools and processes.
3. Engaging others in the whole change process and building commitment.
4. Implementing and sustaining changes: developing effective plans and ensuring that good monitoring and review practices are developed.
5. Facilitating and developing capability: ensuring that people are challenged to find their own answers and that they are supported in doing this.

They proceed to explore the leadership behaviors that tend to be associated with effective change management, content analyzing their evidence (transcripts) to identify emerging themes relating to leadership. These nine categories were identified:

1. What leaders say and do. The communication and actions of leaders related directly to the change.
2. Making others accountable.
3. Thinking about change.
4. Using an individual focus.
5. Establishing "starting points" for change.
6. Designing and managing the change journey.
7. Communicating guiding principles.
8. Creating individual and organizational capabilities.
9. Communicating and creating connections.

Higgs and Rowland (2005, p. 146) found evidence that certain combinations of leadership behaviors appear more effective than others in change situations, in particular (p. 147), approaches referred to as "forming change" and "building capacity." "Shaping behavior," on the other hand, appeared to inhibit the success of change initiatives in all the contexts examined. In their view, this was not surprising in view of developments in the broader leadership literature, which was charting a move from leader-centric, directive behaviors to more facilitating and enabling styles. This would seem to be more consistent with emergent rather than planned approaches to change, as discussed earlier in this report.

Standards for Competence

In addition to the research-based literature, a primary source for information concerning the expected practices and competencies of those in project, program, and change roles can be found in standards. The majority of these standards are primarily guides to the underpinning knowledge and understanding required in an area of practice (e.g., PMI, 2008a; APM, 2006), or best practice guides (e.g., U.K. Cabinet Office, 2011; British Standards Institution, 2010). Competency- or performance-based standards that form part of government-endorsed national qualification frameworks and are designed for an assessment process in which candidates are required to provide evidence that they have carried out the activities identified in the standard are therefore helpful in identifying use of specific practices in the workplace.

Use of practices also appears to be more generic and globally applicable than knowledge, as identified by Crawford and Pollack (2007). There are a number of performance-based standards for project management, including PMI's Competency Development Framework (PMI, 2007), the APM's Competency Framework (APM, 2008), the AIPM's competency standards (Australian Institute of Project Management, 2008) and performance-based standards of the United Kingdom, Australian, and South African governments. The Global Alliance for Project Performance Standards (GAPPS, 2007) has distilled the content of these and other project management standards, including the *PMBOK® Guide* (PMI, 2008a) and the IPMA Competency Baseline (ICB) (International Project Management Association, 2006), into a reduced set of practices expected to be performed by most project managers on most projects.

Performance-based standards are less common for program management and change implementation than they are for project management. While most of the primary standards for project management were developed in the 1990s, standards for program management did not emerge until the late 2000s, the one exception being the U.K. government's *Managing Successful Programmes,* considered to be a "best practice" guide to managing programs. This was first published in 1999 by the Central Computer and Telecommunications Agency (CCTA), which subsequently became part of the Office of Government Commerce (OGC). Further versions were published in 2003 and 2007 by the OGC, and a 2011 version was released under the auspices of the U.K. Cabinet Office (2011).

The Project Management Institute first published *The Standard for Program Management* in 2006, with the second edition released in 2008. The Australian Institute of Project Management has published competency standards for project directors (Australian Institute of Project Management, 2011), which include a statement that at the "Project Director level the individual's primary role is program management" (p. 1), but as the name implies, these standards are still largely focused on the project and are very similar to standards for project managers. The GAPPS published performance-based standards for program managers in 2011.

These standards have eight units of which five, including leadership, stakeholder engagement, crafting the program, realization of benefits, and sustaining program progress, are considered to apply to most program managers in most programs. It is interesting that management of organizational change is one of three sets of practices expected of only some program managers. The other two non-core units relate to management of contracts and engagement in collaborative alliances. There is a close correspondence between the competencies and practices expected of project and program managers, particularly in the areas of planning, monitoring and controlling, and closing. However, while project managers are generally expected to carry out these functions, program managers are generally expected to provide an overseeing role, coordinating the execution of multiple projects. The areas of significant difference, in the standards, between what is expected of project and program managers are that benefits realization, as mentioned earlier in this report, which is considered a core activity of program managers, but not of project managers, and program managers are more likely than project managers to be responsible for management of organizational change.

Although organizational behavior and development have a rich theoretical and research base, there has been significantly less professional formation than there has been for the project management field. The U.K. Office of Government Commerce in their *Successful Delivery Skills Framework* (2004) includes reference to change implementation related activities, and the Change Management Institute (CMI) has developed a set of change management competencies (CMI, 2008), in a format similar to performance-based standards. As the CMI competencies were developed by practitioners in the field of change implementation, they may be considered indicative of expected change implementation practices. It is interesting to note that one of the 11 skill topic areas identified by the CMI is project management:

1. Facilitating change
2. Strategic thinking
3. Thinking and judgment
4. Influencing others
5. Coaching for change
6. Project management
7. Communication
8. Self-management
9. Facilitation—meetings and workshops
10. Professional development
11. Specialist expertise
    a. Learning and development
    b. Communication

Conclusion

As noted by Eskerod (2010, p. 353), even though in the project management literature (Lehtonen & Martinsuo, 2008; Turner et al., 1996) projects and programs are considered vehicles for planned change, research on how to combine change implementation and project and program management has only been carried out to a limited extent (Gareis & Huemann, 2008). If projects and programs are indeed to be so employed, it is important (Gareis, 2010) to define the relevant roles for the change (e.g., owner, manager, and agent) and for the project/program (e.g., owner, manager, and team member). A further consideration is the nature of practices that need to be carried out in the various roles to ensure the success of organizational change projects and of other project types that in many cases require certain changes to be implemented if they are to deliver the desired outcomes and benefits.

Current literature only reports to a limited extent on the roles, practices, and competencies necessary for the successful implementation of change. The focus of the change management literature and the organizational behavior and development field has been on the content and process of change rather than its management. For change implementation, professional formation is in its infancy. By contrast, the project management field is professionally well-developed but may be considered constrained by its own standards to a rational-linear and control-focused view that largely ignores the complex and emergent characteristics associated with implementation of necessary and desirable change. A further gap in this evolving field is investigation and understanding of the relationship between organizational change and project management and between change, project, and program managers. The research reported here was designed to address this gap. The following section outlines the specific questions that drive the research and the research methodology designed to arrive at answers.

Chapter 3

Methodology

Research Aims and Outcomes

As outlined earlier in this document, the aims of this research project are to provide insight into these:

a. the nature of organizational and behavioral change related activities associated with the management of projects/programs
b. the nature of project/program management related activities associated with the management of organizational change projects
c. the extent to which such activities vary relative to the type of project/program, context, and degree of organizational and behavioral change involved
d. patterns of relative involvement of those with project management, organizational development, and other backgrounds in the management of organizational change projects and the organizational and behavioral change related activities associated with projects

Investigation was not limited to projects considered to be organizational change projects but encompassed all project types on the assumption that the majority of projects involve some degree of organizational and/or behavioral change (Buchanan, 1991; Söderlund, 2010).

Potential practical uses for the results are to provide:

- Research-based suggestions for additions to PMI standards;
- Guidance for decision making concerning the management and resourcing of projects responding to the type of project, context, and degree of organizational and behavioral change involved;
- Guidance for leaders/managers in terms of their role relative to organizational change and other project types;
- Guidance for development of role descriptions that recognize change management requirements; and
- Guidance for training and development of project, program, and change managers.

To guide the research in addressing the initial aims and providing practical results for use by professional associations and practitioners, the following questions have been developed.

Project, program, and change related practices

1. What is the nature of project, program, and change related practices associated with the management of projects?

Relationship between nature of the project, practitioner role, and background and use of project, program, and change practices

Nature of the project

2. Does use of project, program, and change related practices vary relative to the **degree of organizational and behavioral change** involved?
3. Does use of project, program, and change related practices vary between projects conducted in **public and private sector organizations**?
4. Does use of project, program, and change related practices vary between projects conducted in **finance and services and engineering sectors**?
5. Does use of project, program, and change related practices vary between projects conducted **for internal and external clients**?
6. Does use of project, program, and change related practices vary between projects of different levels of **complexity**?

Role and background of the practitioner

7. Does use of project, program, and change related practices vary according to role?
8. Does use of project, program, and change related practices vary between practitioners according to age?
9. Does use of project, program, and change related practices vary between practitioners according to gender?
10. Does use of project, program, and change related practices vary between practitioners with different educational backgrounds (PM or CM, etc.)?
11. Does use of project, program, and change related practices vary between practitioners according to length and type of experience (PM/CM/other)?
12. Is there a difference in levels of underpinning project management and change implementation knowledge between roles?

Finally, an interesting and important practical question is whether the use of any of these project and change related practices has an impact on the likelihood of project success. To address this situation, we have one more research question:

Relationship between use of project, program, and change implementation practices and project success

13. Can use of any project, program, and change related practices be identified as predictors of perceived likelihood of **project success**?

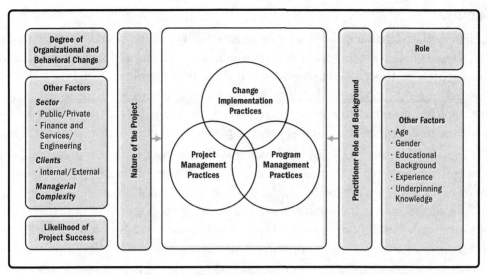

Figure 3-1. Research model - use of project, program, and change related practices according to the nature of the projects and practitioner role and background

Research Design

This research project was designed to build on the qualitative, case study research reported in Crawford and Hassner-Nahmias (2010), which suggested that "project and program managers do not necessarily have the required competence or perform the full activities required to promote and implement the changes that they are leading as part of their projects" (pp. 410–411). Drawing on the project and change implementation literatures and three case studies of IT enabled change, Crawford and Hassner-Nahmias (2010) provide a comparative analysis of the practices and expected competencies of project, program, and change managers finding both similarities and differences.

It was considered that a positivist approach with a quantitative design would provide an opportunity to test findings of previous research while extending it to address a wider range of project types requiring varying degrees of organizational and behavioral change.

The approach taken was to ask those in project, program, and change roles to report on their use of project management and change implementation practices on current or recently completed projects using an online questionnaire. The aim was to seek respondents through project management and change implementation professional associations and through the contacts of the researchers to provide a convenience sample. To encourage completion of the questionnaire, respondents were offered a confidential report on their own project and change management competencies relative to global standards. This was generated and provided to them when they completed the questionnaire online.

Sample

Although the initial approach was to attract individual respondents through the project and change implementation professional associations and through contacts of the researchers, this proved to be extremely difficult. Experience with this and other research projects indicates that it is becoming increasingly difficult to get people to complete questionnaires even where there is an immediate benefit, such as the feedback report provided for those who completed the questionnaire for this project.

To overcome this challenge and gather sufficient data for meaningful analysis, an approach was made to organizations, asking them to arrange participation of 10 or more of their staff in the study. If 10 or more people from one organization completed the survey, the organization would receive a corporate report that would preserve confidentiality of individual results but would identify group strengths and weaknesses in terms of underpinning knowledge and applied skills in project and change management compared to a global average. Use of project and change management practices was reported for knowledge and overall application. For large samples, reporting was, on request, provided by role. A copy of the invitation to organizations is included as Appendix A.

Despite the excellent connections of the researchers and considerable interest from the many organizations approached, the response was disappointing. However, a convenience sample of 180 respondents was finally achieved. As the questionnaire did not require all items to be completed, only 160 of these respondents provided project data.

A limitation of the sample is that despite efforts to achieve a globally representative sample, 155 of the 160 valid responses are from people based in Australia and only 5 from elsewhere (Canada, India, Indonesia, Mexico). It is interesting that although the questionnaire was promoted at conferences of project management professional associations in both Europe and the United States, and requests were made directly to organizations in those regions, no responses were received despite offers and promises to do so. One benefit of this result, and the predominance of responses from individuals in organizations known to the researchers, is that the researchers have a good understanding of the nature and context of respondents. This is helpful in data interpretation.

Although the sample was specifically NOT restricted to those involved in what might be termed organizational change projects, the nature of the survey, both topic and method of securing responses, suggests that there is likely to be a bias towards attraction of respondents who are working on projects involving relatively high levels of organizational change.

According to the research design, the survey was to be completed by those in project, program, and change roles. Change roles were expected to include not only those with the title of change manager but also those in human resource management, communications, and other change related roles. In practice, a distinct subset of change roles emerged, being that of the business analyst. This was not surprising, as previous research (Crawford & Hassner-Nahmias, 2010) had identified that process analysis and design are expected activities in change roles. While the business analyst role can be considered a change role, it has emerged over the last decade as a specialist role with its own defined body of knowledge (IIBA, 2009) and competency model (IIBA, 2011). It was decided therefore to remove the 20 analysts from the dataset that forms the basis for this study.

Therefore, this gives a sample profile as shown in Table 3-1.

Table 3-1. Sample by role

Role	Frequency	Percent
Project roles	78	55.7
Program roles	37	26.4
Change roles	25	17.9
Total	**140**	**100.0**

Of the 140 valid responses, 66 percent are male and 34 percent are female, which is in line with the distribution in other project management related studies. For comparison, the PMI 2010 Member Satisfaction survey had 67 percent responses from males and 33 percent responses from females.[1] The age distribution of the sample is evenly distributed but slightly skewed toward the 35 and over age groups (as shown in Table 3-2).

Table 3-2. Age distribution of sample

Age	Frequency	Percent
25 – 35	36	25.7
35 – 45	54	38.6
Over 45	50	35.7
Total	**140**	**100.0**

Another interesting aspect of the sample is the industry distribution: Thirty-six percent of the sample work in the public or government sector, and 64 percent work in the private sector. Two broad sectors of industry dominate the sample. Sixty percent of all respondents can be categorized as working in the finance and service sectors, and 36 percent are involved in engineering. The dominance of the finance and service sector is not surprising as it is a sector subject to significant business change. It was interesting to find that the engineering sector has recognized the importance of change implementation in what they refer to as the need to ensure "operational readiness."

---

[1]Source: PMI Marketing Department, personal communication, 14 February 2011.

Data Collection Instruments

As indicated in Figure 2-1, to respond to the research questions, data were required to represent:

1. Use of project, program, and change implementation practices
2. Nature of the project
   a. Degree of organizational and behavioral change
   b. Sector
      i. Public or private sector
      ii. Finance and services or engineering
   c. Client
      i. Internal
      ii. External
   d. Managerial Complexity
3. Role and background of the practitioner
   a. Role
   b. Age and gender
   c. Educational background
   d. Experience
   e. Underpinning knowledge
4. Likelihood of project success

The following sections describe the instruments designed to elicit this data to enable analysis.

Use of Project, Program, and Change Implementation Practices

To examine the use of project, program, and change implementation practices, it is necessary to determine what those practices might be. Performance-based standards are helpful in identifying use of specific practices in the workplace because they are designed for an assessment process in which the candidate is required to provide evidence that they have carried out the activities identified in the standard.

There are a number of standards for project management, developed in this format, including the Project Management Institute's Competency Development Framework (PMI, 2007), the APM's Competency Framework (APM, 2008), the AIPM's competency standards (Australian Institute of Project Management, 2008), and performance-based standards of the United Kingdom, Australian, and South African governments.

At commencement of the design and data collection of this research, there were no performance-based standards or equivalent for program management. However, the OGC's (2007) *Managing Successful Programmes* was available and widely used, particularly in the United Kingdom, and PMI's (2008) *The Standard for Program Management* had recently become available. The performance-based standards for program managers produced by the Global Alliance for Project Performance Standards (2011) were not available at the time data collection for this project commenced.

The competencies of the Change Management Institute (CMI) (2008), developed by change implementation practitioners and in a format similar to performance-based standards, provided a good basis for identification of change implementation practices. Business analyst competencies may also be considered relevant to the practices used in change roles.

Table 3-3 provides a summary of the standards and other sources that are available to provide insight into the practices that could be expected to be used in project,

Table 3-3. Summary of sources for identification of project, program, and change implementation practices

Role	Potential Standards	Standard Selected	Instrument Used
Project roles	*AIPM Professional Competency Standards for Project Management* (AIPM, 2008)	*A Framework for Performance Based Competency Standards for Global Level 1 and 2 Project Managers* (GAPPS, 2007)	Self-assessment against 26 items
	National Diploma: Project Management NQF Level 05 (SAQA, 2010)	21 items	
	BSB51407 Diploma of Project Management (IBSA, 2009)		
	National Occupational Standards for Project Management Version 1.01 (ECITB, 2003)		
	A Framework for Performance Based Competency Standards for Global Level 1 and 2 Project Managers (GAPPS, 2007)		
Program roles	*The Standard for Program Management* (PMI, 2008b)	*Managing Successful Programmes* (U.K. Cabinet Office, 2011) (part only)	
	Managing Successful Programmes (UK Cabinet Office, 2011)	5 items	
	A Framework for Performance Based Competency Standards for Program Managers (GAPPS, 2011)		
Change roles	*Change Management Practitioner Competencies* (CMI, 2008)	*Change Management Practitioner Competencies* (CMI, 2008)	Self-assessment against 42 items
	Business Analysis Competency Model Version 3.0 (IIBA, 2011)	42 items	
Total			**Self-assessment against a total of 68 items**

program, and change roles. It also indicates the standard selected as a basis for design of the data collection instrument.

For project and program roles, the GAPPS performance-based standards at the element level were selected for use in collection of data on use of practices. The rationale for this was that these standards draw upon all the other standards, are intentionally generic and global in application, and are the simplest in format and wording. They offer a reduced set of practices expected to be performed by most project managers on most projects. Due to the amount of data being collected, and the broad spectrum of potential respondents, it was necessary to use an instrument that was as brief as possible and used terminology that would be widely and readily understood. The GAPPS (2007) Project Manager Standards have 21 elements, grouped into six units. All 21 elements were used as provided in the standard (see Appendix B).

As a source of expected change related practices there was really no alternative to the competencies of the CMI (2008). For data collection purposes, these Change Management Practitioner Competencies were reduced to 10 skill topic areas/units comprising 42 elements. The content of the original competencies was preserved as far as possible. The following changes were made in the interests of face validity, to ensure that the items used represented practices that could be observed to be used or applied in the workplace and minimize the time involved in completing the research instrument:

- Statements were combined where there was overlap of meaning.
- Original Skill Topic Area 6: Project management was removed, as this is covered by the Project Management Practices data collection instrument.
- Original Skill Topic Area 8: Self-management was removed, as this primarily contained personal behaviors rather than observable practices.
- Skill Topic Area 11: Specialist Expertise was broken into its constituent parts to create Specialist Expertise: Learning and Development and Specialist Expertise: Communication.

The resulting 10 skill topic areas/units are shown in Table 3-4 (items 8 to 17), and the detail of the 42 constituent elements are shown in Appendix C.

Previous research (Crawford & Hassner-Nahmias, 2010) and examination of the OGC's (2007) *Managing Successful Programmes* and PMI's (2008b) *Standard for Program Management* indicated that many program management practices are similar to those of project managers, although they may be considered to differ in level and quality of application. It should be noted that Hassner-Nahmias (2009) was unable to separate project and program roles in practice because the terms and titles tended to be used interchangeably. There was only one area of program management practice, namely, benefits realization (Crawford & Hassner-Nahmias, 2010; OGC, 2007), that was not addressed in some way

Table 3-4. Original grouping of 68 elements used for collection of data on use of project, program, and change related practices

Project and Program Management Practices	Change Management Practices
1. Managing stakeholder relationships (G)	8. Facilitating change (C)
2. Managing development of the plan for the project (G)	9. Strategic thinking (C)
3. Managing project progress (G)	10. Thinking and judgment (C)
4. Managing product acceptance (G)	11. Influencing others (C)
5. Managing project transitions (G)	12. Coaching for change (C)
6. Evaluating and improving project (G)	13. Communication (C)
7. Benefits realization and sustainability performance (MSP)	14. Facilitation of meetings and workshops (C)
	15. Professional development (C)
	16. Specialist expertise: learning and development (C)
	17. Specialist expertise: communications (C)

in performance-based standards for project management or in the CMI's change practitioner competencies. Drawing on *Managing Successful Programmes* (OGC, 2007), five additional elements were added dealing with benefits realization practices.

Data on use of project, program, and change implementation practices were therefore collected against 68 elements drawn from the GAPPS (G) standards (21 elements), *Managing Successful Programmes* (MSP) (5 elements), and the CMI (C) standards (42 elements). These 68 elements were initially grouped into 17 units based on the way in which they were grouped in their parent standards (as shown in Table 3-4).

The scale used for assessment of level of use of practices was based on that used in previous studies (Crawford, 2005; Aitken & Crawford, 2008), modified for the specific purposes of this research. Participants were asked to describe two of their most recent projects. They were then asked to think about those two projects and rate each of the 68 elements on the following five-point Likert scale:

1. I did not do this on either of the projects I described.
2. I did this as a team member under supervision on one or both of the projects I described.
3. I did this myself on one of the projects I described.
4. I did this myself on both of the projects I described.
5. I did not do this myself, but I managed others doing this on one or both of the projects I described.

This scale is useful for self-assessment and for the aims of this research as it does not ask respondents to make a subjective judgment about how well they carry out the various activities; they merely need to report whether they used the practices and if so at which level.

Further, as respondents were assured that the results were confidential and that they would receive a report providing recommendations for professional development, they were further encouraged to report as honestly as possible. A limitation is that all respondents may not interpret the elements in the same way, but the researchers' previous use of this scale has indicated that it provides a good representation of the level of usage of workplace practices.

Mean scores for use of project, program, and change related practices, at unit level, are shown in Table 3-5. The source of each unit is shown as follows: GAPPS (G), Change Management Institute (C), and *Managing Successful Programmes* (M). The reliability and internal consistency of all units can be considered good (Cronbach's Alpha>0.80) to excellent (Cronbach's Alpha>0.90), as shown in Table 3-5.

Grouping of the 68 elements as they appear in their source documents is useful for analysis of use of practices in terms of current professional expectations for project and change roles. However, there is significant overlap between the

Table 3-5. Mean scores for use of project, program, and change related practices

	Practice Sets	Source	N	Minimum	Maximum	Mean	Standard Deviation	Cronbach's Alpha
1	Manage stakeholder relationships	G	140	1	5	3.54	0.823	0.825
2	Plan the project	G	140	1	5	3.44	0.959	0.896
3	Manage project progress	G	138	1	5	3.45	0.955	0.878
4	Manage product acceptance	G	138	1	5	3.46	1.041	0.932
5	Manage project transitions	G	139	1	5	3.29	1.001	0.847
6	Evaluate and improve performance	G	138	1	5	3.05	1.128	0.903
7	Benefits realization	M	139	1	5	2.94	1.206	0.927
8	Facilitating change	C	140	1	5	3.33	1.140	0.899
9	Strategic thinking	C	140	1	5	3.19	1.178	0.868
10	Thinking and judgment	C	140	1	5	3.78	0.758	0.835
11	Influencing others	C	140	1	5	3.55	0.757	0.769
12	Coaching for change	C	140	1	5	3.25	1.123	0.867
13	Communication	C	139	1	5	3.65	0.771	0.864
14	Facilitation of meetings and workshops	C	139	1	5	3.67	0.834	0.896
15	Professional development	C	140	1	5	2.86	1.227	0.834
16	Specialist expertise: learning and development	C	139	1	5	3.27	1.256	0.894
17	Specialist expertise: communications	C	138	1	5	3.36	1.239	0.943

expectations of what will be done in the three areas of practice (project, program, change). For example, communications and stakeholder relationships are mentioned in both the project manager and change manager competencies, although with slightly different terminology. For this reason, the 68 elements were subsequently thematically grouped, for purposes of analysis, into 14 units that reflected the evidence from previous studies (Crawford & Hassner-Nahmias, 2010) and the control and process agendas proposed by Buchanan (1991). These are presented in Table 3-6. As with the original or standards-based grouping, there is good internal validity to these scales (Cronbach's Alpha for each item shown in Table 3-6).

Table 3-6. Reliability of derived scales for project, program, and change practice

Practice Sets	Source	Number of Items	N	Minimum	Maximum	Mean	Standard Deviation	Cronbach's Alpha
CONTROL AGENDA		17						
Plan the project	PM	6	140	1.00	5.00	3.44	0.942	0.910
Monitor and control progress	PM	4	138	1.00	5.00	3.50	0.949	0.920
Manage project transitions	PM	3	139	1.00	5.00	3.29	1.001	0.847
Realize benefits	ProgM	4	139	1.00	5.00	2.92	1.210	0.911
PROCESS AGENDA		51						
Plan and facilitate change	CI	5	140	1.00	5.00	3.25	1.151	0.884
Engage stakeholders	PM/CI	8	140	1.00	5.00	3.54	0.757	0.863
Manage communications	PM/CI	9	140	1.00	5.00	3.58	0.845	0.906
Communicate change	CI	3	140	1.00	5.00	3.18	1.189	0.765
Prepare users	CI	7	140	1.00	5.00	3.20	1.187	0.912
Build support	CI	4	140	1.00	5.00	3.60	0.729	0.799
Ensure business integration	CI	4	140	1.00	5.00	3.22	1.059	0.810
Make informed decisions	CI	3	140	1.00	5.00	3.78	0.758	0.835
Demonstrate self-awareness	CI	3	139	1.00	5.00	3.10	1.038	0.771
Evaluate and improve performance	PM	5	140	1.00	5.00	3.12	1.020	0.865
TOTAL NUMBER OF ITEMS		**68**						

Planning the project, monitoring and controlling progress, managing project transitions (life cycle), and realization of benefits have been identified as representing a control agenda. The balance of the practices are more concerned with process. Planning and facilitating change and communicating change, although related to planning the project and managing communications, reflect a specific focus on change implementation, while a number of the other elements, although drawing on practices from both project and change implementation, are more generic in their application. Although the skill topic area of self-management, which is present in the original CMI Competencies (CMI, 2008), was removed for data collection purposes (see explanation earlier in the chapter), three of the remaining elements used for data collection purposes were re-categorized under a new but similar heading of Demonstrate Self-Awareness. The full set of 68 elements, grouped into the units shown in Table 3-6, is provided in Appendix E: Thematic Grouping of Units for Project, Program, and Change Practice.

Nature of the Project

a) Degree of Organizational and Behavioral Change

For the two recent projects they had described, the study participants were asked to indicate the degree of organizational and behavioral change required in each project on a four-point Likert scale, from low to very high. The following descriptor of organizational and behavioral change was provided to assist respondents in making their assessment.

> *Most projects have an element of change to them. This can be either behavioral i.e. staff impacted by the project are required to do something differently or organizational i.e. the organization has to operate in a different way. The degree of change can be identified by the number of people affected by the change, the extent of changes to the way the work is performed, the number of business areas affected, the influence on the organization as a whole.*

The mean score from the two projects was selected to represent the degree of organizational and behavioral change on projects in which the participant is generally involved. The low and medium scores were combined, providing a trivariate variable with good distribution (see Table 3-7).

Table 3-7. Degree of organizational and behavioral change required on projects

DEGREE OF ORGANIZATIONAL AND BEHAVIORAL CHANGE				
Valid	**Frequency**	**Percent**	**Valid Percent**	**Cumulative Percent**
Low to medium	45	32.1	32.1	32.1
High	44	31.4	31.4	63.6
Very high	51	36.4	36.4	100.0
Total	**140**	**100.0**	**100.0**	

b) Sector

As discussed earlier, the sample distribution by sector is 37 percent in the public or government sector and 63 percent in the private sector across two broad industry sectors, which can be categorized as finance and service sectors (64 percent) and engineering (36 percent). The combined sector distribution is shown in Table 3-8.

Table 3-8. Sector distribution of sample

PUBLIC/PRIVATE SECTOR – INDUSTRY SECTOR CROSSTABULATION			
	Industry Sector		
Sector	Finance and Services	Engineering	Total
Public	14	37	51
Private	70	19	89
Total	84	56	140

c) Client

Besner and Hobbs (2008) found that projects are managed quite differently for internal and external customers. It can also be expected that the majority of organizational change projects will be managed on behalf of internal clients. This was therefore considered a potentially useful project characteristic to include in analysis. It is interesting to note that while in both the finance and services and engineering sectors the majority of projects are undertaken for internal clients, there is an even balance in engineering but a significant bias towards internal clients in finance and services.

Table 3-9. Sample by industry sector and internal or external client

CLIENT TYPE – INDUSTRY SECTOR CROSSTABULATION			
	Industry Sector		
Client Type	Finance and Services	Engineering	Total
External	8	26	34
Internal	76	30	106
Total	84	56	140

d) Managerial Complexity

Complexity is one of the most common attributes used to categorize projects (Crawford et al., 2006). It is also reasonable to assume that higher degrees of organizational and behavioral change will be associated with increasing levels of managerial complexity. To test this assumption and to provide further contextual understanding of the use of project and change management practices, respondents were asked to briefly describe two of their most recent projects and to provide an indication of the level of managerial complexity of these projects on seven dimensions. These seven dimensions were based on the CIFTER table used in association with the GAPPS (2007) performance-based standards to determine the level of evidence that a project manager would be able to provide to support competency claims.

Previous research by Aitken and Crawford (2007), using these dimensions of managerial complexity and comparing self-assessed project ratings with ratings for the same projects by independent assessors, found a high level of agreement. Although the ratings may be considered both subjective and relative, the self-ratings and those of independent assessors were the same in 84 percent of cases. Further, unpublished research by the authors, working with a financial institution to assess the managerial complexity of their portfolio of projects has indicated similar results.

As respondents provided ratings of managerial complexity for two recent projects, the average of the rating for the two projects was used. Descriptive statistics of the managerial complexity ratings are presented in Table 3-10. A full description of the seven dimensions is provided in Appendix F.

To provide a single score to represent the level of managerial complexity of projects worked on by the respondents, the mean scores for all seven dimensions were added together and averaged. The higher the score, the higher the level of managerial complexity.[2]

Table 3-10. Seven dimensions of managerial complexity of projects (presented in descending order of means)

	N	Minimum	Maximum	Mean	Standard Deviation
Strategic importance	139	1.00	4.00	3.3957	0.60933
Organizational interfaces	139	1.00	4.00	3.0683	0.64606
Stakeholder cohesion	140	1.00	4.00	3.0464	0.65398
Number of disciplines and methods	139	1.00	4.00	2.7374	0.74292
Financial impact	136	1.00	4.00	2.6618	0.74008
Stability of context	140	1.00	4.00	2.6286	0.64699
Legal, social, environmental implications	140	1.00	4.00	2.3000	0.86040

[2]Note that values for stability of context and stakeholder cohesion were reversed to derive the score for overall project complexity, as higher levels of stability and cohesion would be associated with lower levels of complexity.

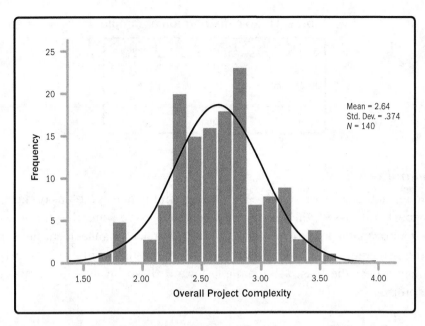

Figure 3-2. Histogram of overall project complexity

Role and Background of the Practitioner

a) Role

Role of the respondent was one of the key items in the data collection and has been discussed earlier in this paper in describing the research design and sample for the study. Participants were asked to select their current role from a set of five predetermined role categories (project manager, project director, program manager, change manager, other) and also to state the actual title of their role. The rationale for using this set of predetermined role categories, rather than just proposing project, program, and change manager roles, is that experience of the researchers indicates that there are, in practice, a wide range of job titles. Individuals completing questionnaires are often unclear as to where they fit, and it is important to provide them with options to avoid frustration. As there is no clear definition of change roles and project/ program roles (Stummer & Zuchi, 2010) and as the sample was drawn from a broad range of participants across change, general, and project management communities, it is interesting but not surprising that 44 percent of the sample selected "other" as the category for their current role. As was initially intended, those reporting project director roles were re-categorized to program manager roles. Examination of role titles, examination of project descriptions, and experience of the researchers enabled re-categorization of those listed as "other" to form the categories as presented in Table 3-11.

Table 3-11. Role distribution of sample

Role	Frequency	Percent
Project roles	78	55.7
Program roles	37	26.4
Change roles	25	17.9
Total	**140**	**100.0**

b) Age and Gender

Data on age and gender were collected to establish the demographics of the sample. As previously discussed, the results for this sample were generally in line with expected demographics for research studies in the project management field. If anything, the percentage of female respondents was very slightly higher than expected, which may reflect the bias of the sample toward those involved in organizational change projects.

Table 3-12: Age and gender distribution of sample

Age	Frequency	Percent	Gender	Frequency	Percent
25 – 35	36	25.7	Male	92	65.7
35 – 45	54	38.6			
Over 45	50	35.7	Female	48	34.3
Total	**140**	**100.0**	**Total**	**140**	**100.0**

c) Educational Background

As educational background and relevant professional certification may be expected to influence a number of factors including understanding of the role, underpinning knowledge, and awareness and use of practices, respondents were asked to indicate their level of post-school education and whether they held any professional certifications in project management.

Table 3-13. Postgraduate degrees held by respondents (N=140)

Postgraduate Qualifications	N
Graduate Certification in Change Management	2
Master's Degree in PM	9
Other Master's Degree	9
MBA	15
PhD	1
Total with postgraduate qualifications	**36**

Seventy-one percent of respondents have a first degree, and 24 percent have one or more postgraduate qualifications. The nature of these postgraduate qualifications is shown in Table 3-13. None of the respondents reported holding more than one postgraduate qualification.

Thirty-five percent of the sample indicated that they held one or more project management professional certifications, and the breakdown of certifications held is shown in Table 3-14. Of the PMI certifications, only one was a Certified Associate in Project Management (CAPM)®. Ten respondents hold more than one project management certification. Of these, one holds both a Project Management Professional (PMP)® and a PRINCE2 qualification, and four hold a PRINCE2 qualification plus either an AIPM CPPP, CPPM, or CPPD or the equivalent AQF (Australian Qualifications Framework) qualification.

Table 3-14. Project management certifications held by respondents (*N*=140)

Project Management Certifications	N
PMI Certification (CAPM® or PMP®)	15
AIPM CPPP or Cert IV in PM (AQF)	13
AIPM CPPM or Dip in PM (AQF)	19
AIPM CPPD or Adv Dip in PM (AQF)	4
PRINCE2	15

To provide a basis for further analysis, the various qualifications and certifications held by respondents were synthesized. Table 3-15 presents a summary of the highest level of academic and professional certification of all respondents. Notably, only 13 percent of the sample have no qualifications or certifications, and only 8 percent have a professional certification.

Table 3-15. Highest level of academic and professional qualifications

Highest Qualification Level	Frequency	Percent
No Qualifications	18	12.9
PM Certification only	11	7.9
Undergraduate Degree only	54	38.6
Postgraduate Degree only (includes Undergraduate)	19	13.6
Undergraduate Degree and PM Certification	24	17.1
Postgraduate Degree and PM Certification	14	10.0
Total	**140**	**100.0**

d) Experience

Much learning and habituation of practice comes from experience. Experience can also be expected to influence the perspectives of practitioners. To provide insight into the influence that experience might have on use of project and change management practices, respondents were asked to indicate number of years of experience in:

- Project management
- Change management
- A number of other practice domains

Table 3-16. Project management and change management experience

Experience	N	Percent	Minimum	Maximum	Mean (Years of Experience)	Standard Deviation
Project management experience (years)	137	92.0	0	39	10.72	7.521
Change management experience (years)	133	65.0	0	33	5.23	6.160

As can be seen in Table 3-16, nearly all respondents (92 percent) claim some experience in project management, and a majority of respondents (65 percent) claim to have experience in change management. Table 3-17 provides further assistance in interpreting these results. Thirty-nine respondents claim only project management experience, and two, with the role of change manager, claim only change management experience. Those who claim neither project nor change management experience are engineers (2) and HRM/operations (5). As answers to the questions relating to experience were not mandatory, and as these seven respondents provided data on projects in which they had been involved, they were retained in the sample and this item was treated as missing data.

Table 3-17. Details of project and change management experience

Experience	Frequency	Percent
Only PM experience	39	27.9
Only CM experience	2	1.4
Both PM and CM experience	92	65.7
Missing data	7	5.0
Total	**140**	**100.0**

As shown in Table 3-16, the average experience in project management is 10 years and the average for change management is 4.9 years. The range of project and change management experience is shown in Figures 3-3 and 3-4.

Experience in practice domains included information technology, engineering and construction, sales, communications and marketing, human resource management, organizational development, and business process re-engineering. Experience in

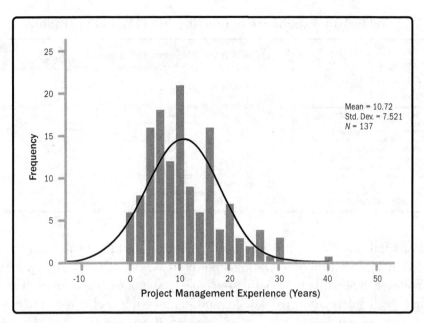

Figure 3-3. Histogram of project management experience (years)

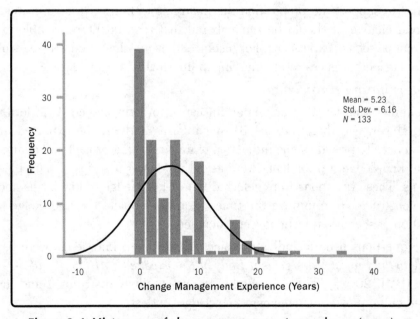

Figure 3-4. Histogram of change management experience (years)

Table 3-18. Experience in practice domains and operations

	N	Percent	Minimum	Maximum	Mean (Years of Experience)	Standard Deviation
Information technology	94	0.59	0	37	12.82	9.083
Operations/BAU	70	0.44	0	30	7.89	7.021
Business process reengineering (BPR)	64	0.40	0	23	6.27	5.134
Engineering and construction	47	0.29	0	43	13.55	12.397
Organizational development	37	0.23	0	30	5.32	6.205
Human resource management	35	0.22	0	30	5.57	6.317
Sales	31	0.19	0	30	4.61	5.993
Communications and marketing	26	0.16	0	20	4.46	5.391

operations (business as usual) was also nominated. Details of this experience are provided in Table 3-18 in descending order of frequency of report. It is interesting to note, however, that while information technology and operations are most frequently reported, both information technology and engineering and construction have the highest average number of years of experience at around 13 years. The relatively high incidence (40 percent of the sample) of experience in business process re-engineering, which is directly related to organizational change, is interesting. When read in conjunction with the predominance of project roles (56 percent of the sample), this tends to support the proposition that many projects involve organizational and behavioral change. It should be remembered that respondents were able to report concurrent periods of experience. For instance, they may have had five years of experience of business process re-engineering in information technology.

e) Underpinning Knowledge

Underpinning knowledge is an important aspect of competence (Crawford, 2005; Gonczi, Hager, & Athanasou, 1993) that informs and can be expected to influence practice. To provide some indication of underpinning project and change management knowledge, respondents were asked to answer a series of multiple-choice questions. These questions were selected to test knowledge of key terms and theoretical constructs. To minimize the time taken to complete the knowledge test, no calculation or scenario questions were included.

The questions used to indicate project management knowledge were based on *A Guide to the Project Management Body of Knowledge (PMBOK® Guide)*—Fourth Edition (PMI, 2008a). This is arguably the most widely distributed and therefore accepted of the project management knowledge guides.

Identifying a source upon which to base change management knowledge questions was more challenging, as at the time of designing the research, there was a change management knowledge guide similar to those available for project management. As the actual project management body of knowledge extends well beyond its various "guides," so does the body of knowledge that underpins the implementation of organizational and behavioral change. The body of knowledge is embedded in the many journal articles and texts on organizational development, behavioral science, and associated fields.

To develop a test for underpinning change management knowledge, a decision was therefore made to base questions on a publication that covered the full breadth of the discipline. A text used in academic programs teaching organizational development and behavioral science seemed appropriate, as it would represent the accepted knowledge in the field.

The researchers therefore developed criteria for choosing the publication upon which the change management knowledge test would be developed:

- Published within the past five years
- Authored by academics
- Used as a text in universities
- Each chapter covers change related topics consistently and in depth
- Each chapter deals with an aspect of change management rather than exploring a single aspect of the discipline throughout the publication
- Topics covered can be seen to relate to the thinking that drives the change management competencies identified by the Change Management Institute

After reviewing several publications for their alignment to the criteria, the publication chosen by the researchers was *Managing Organizational Change* (Graetz, Rimmer, Smith, & Lawrence, 2006). This publication responded positively to the criteria. A third edition was released in 2010.

The knowledge test questions followed the book chapters. At least one question was developed per chapter. In each chapter, the researchers investigated the key messages that the chapter aimed to deliver and used these as the base for the development of the question.

On the basis outlined previously, respondents were asked to answer 20 questions relating to project management and 20 questions relating to organizational change, a total of 40 questions. The results were intended to provide an overall indicator of level of knowledge in each field, so there are only two data items here: a score for change management knowledge and a score for project management knowledge, with a maximum score of 20 in each case. As shown in Table 3-19, the maximum score for both project and change management knowledge was 16/20. The mean is for project management knowledge, which is only very slightly higher than for change management knowledge. Although the mean is relatively low (just below 50 percent of the maximum possible score) for both project and change management knowledge, this is not unexpected. In a similar study where a series of multiple-choice questions were used to provide an indicator of underpinning project management knowledge,

Table 3-19. Results of tests for underpinning project and change implementation knowledge

DESCRIPTIVE STATISTICS					
	N	Minimum	Maximum	Mean	Standard Deviation
Project management knowledge	138	1.00	16.00	9.7391	2.71332
Change implementation knowledge	138	3.00	16.00	9.6594	2.66498

the mean was 56 percent (Crawford, 2001). In both cases, the participants were not prepared in any way to complete the knowledge test.

Likelihood of Project Success

Underpinning interest in the practices used and knowledge applied in the management of projects is an assumption that the right combination will contribute to the likelihood of project success. The research design therefore included the collection of data concerning the participant perceptions of the likelihood of success of the two recent projects they had described. In keeping with Baker, Murphy, and Fisher's (1988) suggestion, a project is most likely to be perceived as successful if:

> . . .the project meets the technical performance specifications and/or mission to be performed, and if there is a high level of satisfaction concerning the project outcome among key people on the project team, and key users or clientele of the project effort. (p. 902)

Study participants were asked to answer the following four questions concerning the two projects they had described. Reponses were requested on a 5-point Likert scale where 1 was "Not likely at all" and 5 was "Definite likelihood."

1. Overall likelihood of the project being perceived as successful by most of the key stakeholders (Stakeholder satisfaction)
2. Likelihood of the project finishing on time (Time performance)
3. Likelihood of the project finishing on budget (Budget performance)
4. Likelihood of delivery of expected benefits (Benefits delivery)

The mean score from the two projects was selected to represent the perceived overall likelihood of success of the projects in which the participant had applied the project, program, and change implementation practices described earlier. The results for the four dimensions of perceived likelihood of project success are shown as histograms in Figure 3-5. As five is the highest score, time performance can be seen as the strongest of these dimensions.

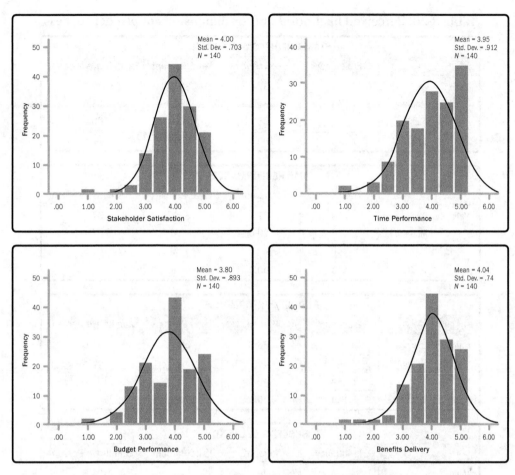

Figure 3-5. Histograms for four dimensions of perceived likelihood of project success

By taking four as a central score, it was possible to derive trivariate variables for each of the four dimensions of likelihood of project success with good distribution as shown in Table 3-20.

Table 3-20. Perceived likelihood of four dimensions of project success

STAKEHOLDER SATISFACTION		Frequency	Percent	Valid Percent	Cumulative Percent
Valid	Low	45	32.1	32.1	32.1
	Medium	44	31.4	31.4	63.6
	High	51	36.4	36.4	100.0
	Total	**140**	**100.0**	**100.0**	

TIME PERFORMANCE		Frequency	Percent	Valid Percent	Cumulative Percent
Valid	Low	52	37.1	37.1	37.1
	Medium	28	20.0	20.0	57.1
	High	60	42.9	42.9	100.0
	Total	**140**	**100.0**	**100.0**	

BUDGET PERFORMANCE		Frequency	Percent	Valid Percent	Cumulative Percent
Valid	Low	54	38.6	38.6	38.6
	Medium	43	30.7	30.7	69.3
	High	43	30.7	30.7	100.0
	Total	**140**	**100.0**	**100.0**	

BENEFITS DELIVERY		Frequency	Percent	Valid Percent	Cumulative Percent
Valid	Low	40	28.6	28.6	28.6
	Medium	45	32.1	32.1	60.7
	High	55	39.3	39.3	100.0
	Total	**140**	**100.0**	**100.0**	

Combining the four dimensions of project success provides a measure of the overall likelihood of perceived success of the projects in which each study participant is involved (see Table 3-21).

Table 3-21. Perceived overall likelihood of project success

		Frequency	Percent	Valid Percent	Cumulative Percent
PROJECT SUCCESS					
Valid	Low	54	38.6	38.6	38.6
	Medium	16	11.4	11.4	50.0
	High	70	50.0	50.0	100.0
	Total	**140**	**100.0**	**100.0**	

Approach to Analysis

Having presented the research questions, the research design, and the variables available for analysis to find answers to these questions, the following sections of this report will present results in the following themes:

- The nature and use of project management and change implementation practices
- The influence of context
- The role and background of the practitioner
- Predictors of project success

Chapter 4

Analysis and Results

Nature and Use of Project Management and Change Implementation Practices

The first challenge of this research was to identify the nature of project management and change implementation practices and the extent to which they are used across a range of projects. As explained in the previous chapter, respondents were asked to rate their level of use of 68 project, program, and change implementation practices on two of their most recent projects. These 68 items were then thematically grouped into 14 sets of practices as a basis for analysis.

To answer the question:

> What is the nature of project management, organizational, and behavioral change related practices associated with the management of projects?

The mean scores of these 14 sets of practices were ranked in descending order of mean level of usage. The results of this analysis are shown in Figure 4-1, which also identifies the source of the practices within the set (project management, change implementation, both project management and change implementation, or program management) and whether the practice set may be considered representative of a control agenda (CA) or process agenda (PA), as suggested by Buchanan (1991).

As can be seen in Figure 4-1, the two sets of practices that are used at the highest level, make informed decisions and build support, are drawn from change implementation and are representative of a process agenda. These are closely followed by two sets of practices that are drawn from both project management and change implementation sources and are again representative of a process agenda. Next come the three most highly used project management practices. Practices relating to benefits realization, drawn from program management, are notably the practices evidencing the lowest level of use in this sample.

These results have a high level of face validity. The four most highly used sets of practices across this sample may be considered generic. These are the types of activities that might be expected of anyone in a management or leadership role, regardless of their specific discipline. They involve engagement with others to achieve results.

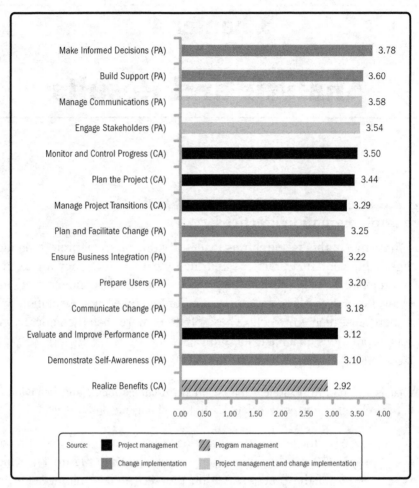

Figure 4-1. Mean scores for practice sets in descending order of level of use
(CA=Control Agenda; PA=Process Agenda [Buchanan, 1991])

This is consistent with Weick's (2001) view that the work of organizations consists of "irrevocable choices that necessitate justification" (p. 3) and Stacey's concept of complex responsive processes of relating, which considers "organization" to be an emergent property of many individual human beings interacting together in a responsive manner (Stacey, 2001; Cicmil et al., 2009).

Both Weick and Stacey recognize, in the process of sensemaking, that people will employ "tools of some kind, in order to express identities and 'earn a living'" (Stacey, 2001, p. 195). This is reflected in the sets of project management (control agenda) and change implementation (process agenda) practices that are next highest in use for this sample. Lower levels of use of evaluation and improvement of performance and realization of benefits are consistent with results from other studies (e.g., Crawford & Cooke-Davies, 2012c).

Nature of the Project

The results in the previous section indicate the overall level of use of project management and change implementation practices but do not indicate whether the level of use of the various practices differs relative to characteristics of the project or its context. The project and context characteristics investigated were:

- Degree of organizational and behavioral change involved
- Sector
  - Public sector vs. private sector
  - Industry sector
- Client: internal or external
- Degree of management complexity of the project

Different statistical techniques were used, according to the nature of the data, to identify differences in use of practices relative to these five characteristics. The results of these analyses are reported in the following section.

Degree of Organizational and Behavioral Change

Analysis of variance (ANOVA) techniques for testing of statistical significant differences were used to answer the second research question:

Does use of project, program, and change related practices vary relative to the **degree of organizational and behavioral change** involved?

Using the variable for degree of behavioral and organizational change of projects worked on by participants (Table 3-7) and the mean scores for use of project, program, and change practices presented in Table 3-5, analysis of variance techniques (ANOVA) (Table 4-1) only shows a significant difference in use of practices at $P<0.05$ level for make informed decisions ($P=0.045$), build support ($P=0.016$), manage communications ($P=0.036$), engage stakeholders ($P=0.014$), prepare users ($P=0.010$), and communicate change ($P=0.038$). As might be expected, all of these practices are carried out at significantly higher levels on projects with very high degrees of organizational and behavioral change than on those considered low to medium or high. Four of these six sets of practices are drawn entirely from the change implementation toolkit, while engage stakeholders and manage communications are drawn from both change implementation and project management. It is worth noting, however, that there is no evidence of difference in use of project management practices relative to degree of organizational and behavioral change.

Table 4-1. Statistically significant differences between use of practices by degree of organizational and behavioral change (ANOVA)

		Sum of Squares	df	Mean Square	F	Significance
Make informed decisions	Between groups	3.536	2	1.768	3.170	0.045
	Within groups	76.413	137	0.558		
	Total	**79.949**	**139**			
Build support	Between groups	4.352	2	2.176	4.283	0.016
	Within groups	69.610	137	0.508		
	Total	**73.962**	**139**			
Manage communications	Between groups	4.702	2	2.351	3.403	0.036
	Within groups	94.648	137	0.691		
	Total	**99.350**	**139**			
Engage stakeholders	Between groups	4.801	2	2.400	4.395	0.014
	Within groups	74.815	137	0.546		
	Total	**79.615**	**139**			
Monitor and control progress	Between groups	1.821	2	0.911	1.011	0.366
	Within groups	121.559	135	0.900		
	Total	**123.381**	**137**			
Plan the project	Between groups	4.307	2	2.154	2.478	0.088
	Within groups	119.066	137	0.869		
	Total	**123.373**	**139**			
Manage project transitions	Between groups	2.820	2	1.410	1.414	0.247
	Within groups	135.588	136	0.997		
	Total	**138.408**	**138**			
Plan and facilitate change	Between groups	5.369	2	2.685	2.057	0.132
	Within groups	178.821	137	1.305		
	Total	**184.190**	**139**			
Ensure business integration	Between groups	3.354	2	1.677	1.505	0.226
	Within groups	152.603	137	1.114		
	Total	**155.957**	**139**			
Prepare users	Between groups	12.812	2	6.406	4.797	0.010
	Within groups	182.960	137	1.335		
	Total	**195.771**	**139**			
Communicate change	Between groups	9.157	2	4.579	3.348	0.038
	Within groups	187.378	137	1.368		
	Total	**196.536**	**139**			
Evaluate and improve performance	Between groups	1.663	2	0.832	0.797	0.453
	Within groups	142.972	137	1.044		
	Total	**144.636**	**139**			
Demonstrate self-awareness	Between groups	3.297	2	1.648	1.542	0.218
	Within groups	145.337	136	1.069		
	Total	**148.633**	**138**			
Realize benefits	Between groups	3.716	2	1.858	1.275	0.283
	Within groups	198.186	136	1.457		
	Total	**201.902**	**139**			

Therefore, in answer to the second question, there is clear evidence of variation in use of project, program, and change practices relative to the degree of organizational and behavioral change of projects. Change implementation practices (make informed decisions, build support, prepare users, and communicate change) and practices common to both change implementation and project management (engage stakeholders and manage communications) are used at higher levels on projects requiring higher degrees of organizational and behavioral change. Of equal interest, however, are those practices where there is clearly no evidence of significant difference ($P<0.1$) relative to degree of organizational and behavioral change: monitor and control progress, manage project transitions, plan and facilitate change, ensure business integration, evaluate and improve performance, demonstrate self-awareness, and realize benefits. As plan and facilitate change, ensure business integration, and demonstrate self-awareness are drawn entirely from the change implementation toolkit, it might have been expected that they would have been used at a higher level on projects requiring higher degrees of organizational and behavioral change.

Sector

Two aspects of projects relating to sector were investigated. First, participants were asked whether they were working on projects in the public or private sector. Second, the participants were drawn from two major industry sectors: finance and business, and engineering and construction. As the independent variables each have only two values, Independent Samples T-Tests were conducted to identify significant differences in use of practices, first in public and private sector contexts and then according to industry sector.

Public vs. Private Sector
Using the variable for public/private sector context (Table 3-8) and the mean scores for use of project, program, and change practices presented in Table 3-5, an Independent Samples T-Test (Appendix G: Independent Samples T-Tests) shows a significant difference between the average for the use of the practices in the public sector and the average for the use of the practices in the private sector in all but one set of practices, namely build support. In all cases, the practices are used at a higher level in the private sector than in the public sector. However, the difference between the means is not significant for build support ($P=0.149$), which is the second most highly used of the practice sets and may also be considered generic to management roles.

In response to the question:

> Does use of project, program, and change related practices vary between projects conducted in **public and private sector organizations**?

We can therefore conclude, for this sample, that there is significant variation in use of all practices except building support. As the differences span both project management and change implementation practices, we may also conclude that this is indicative of a generally lower level of use of all practices within the public sector.

Industry Sector

Using the variable for industry sector context (Table 3-8) and the mean scores for use of project, program, and change practices presented in Table 3-5, an independent samples T-Test (Appendix G: Independent Samples T-Tests) shows significant differences between the averages for use of practices in the finance and business services sector and in engineering and construction in four sets of change implementation practices (plan and facilitate change, ensure business integration, prepare users, and communicate change), one set of practices common to both project management and change implementation (manage communications), and the one set of program management practices, realize benefits. In each case, the practices are used at a higher level in the finance and business services sector than in engineering and construction. One might speculate that the significantly higher use of these change implementation practices in the finance and business services sector reflects a tendency towards projects with higher degrees of organizational and behavioral change. However, analysis of the averages for degree of organizational and behavioral change in the two industry sectors reveals only a slightly higher level of change in the finance and business services sector, and no significance in the difference. This suggests that those working in the finance and business services sector are more likely to use these particular change implementation practices than those in the engineering and construction sector.

The significantly higher use of benefits realization practices in the finance and business services sector is consistent with results from other studies indicating a higher number of projects with intangible rather than tangible outcomes in this sector (Crawford & Cooke-Davies, 2012). Where projects are delivering intangible outcomes, benefits realization provides a means of assessing performance.

From this analysis, the answer to the question:

> Does use of project, program, and change related practices vary between projects conducted in **finance and services and engineering sectors**?

is that, for this sample, there is no significant variation in use of project management practices, or the more generic change implementation practices according to industry sector. realize benefits, and four sets of specific change implementation practices (plan and facilitate change, ensure business integration, prepare users, and communicate change) are used at significantly higher levels in the finance and business services sector than in engineering and construction.

Client

Research supports an assumption that projects will be managed differently for internal and external clients (Besner & Hobbs, 2008), and we may also assume that the majority of organizational and behavioral change projects will be conducted for internal clients. The following research question was therefore posed:

> Does use of project, program, and change related practices vary between projects conducted **for internal and external clients**?

Using the variable for internal and external clients (Table 3-9) and the mean scores for use of project, program, and change practices presented in Table 3-5, an independent samples t test (Appendix G: Independent Samples T-Tests) reveals that there are no significant differences between the averages for use of practices on projects for internal and external clients **except for** make informed decisions and monitor and control progress, which are used at a higher level on projects for external clients than for internal clients. The importance of perceived control on behalf of external clients is consistent with circumstances associated with such projects, which may include contract conditions and desire for repeat business. Although the differences are not significant between use of other practices on projects for internal and external clients, the trend is generally towards higher use of all project management practices on projects for external clients. Specialist change implementation practices (plan and facilitate change, prepare users, and communicate change) and the one set of program management practices, realize benefits, tend to be used at slightly higher levels for internal clients.

Management Complexity

As outlined in the previous chapter, participants were asked to rate their project against seven dimensions representing aspects of management complexity. These ratings were combined to provide an overall rating of project complexity. To answer the question:

> Does use of project, program, and change related practices vary between projects of different levels of **complexity**?

a correlation analysis of the practices (independent variables) and the dependent variables, overall project complexity and its seven component dimensions, was conducted. As shown in Table 4-2, three sets of practice variables were found to be significantly positively correlated ($P<=0.05$) with overall project complexity: build support, manage communications, and demonstrate self-awareness. Demonstration of self-awareness is strongly correlated ($P<0.01$) with overall project complexity and a number of its component dimensions: strategic importance, number of disciplines and methods, and legal, social, and environmental implications. The relationship

Table 4-2. Pearson correlations between use of practices and dimensions of management complexity

	Overall Project Complexity	Strategic Importance	Number of Organizational Interfaces	Stakeholder Cohesion	Number of Disciplines & Methods	Financial Impact	Stability of Context	Legal, Social, Environmental Implications
Make informed decisions	0.104	0.231**	0.087	0.154	0.155	0.146	0.263**	0.140
Build support	0.187*	0.266**	0.136	0.075	0.168*	0.120	0.209*	0.226**
Manage communications	0.172*	0.261**	0.154	0.193*	0.188*	0.150	0.235**	0.255**
Engage stakeholders	0.077	0.268**	0.149	0.182*	0.135	0.051	0.225**	0.080
Monitor and control progress	0.089	0.232**	0.102	0.129	0.047	0.058	0.091	0.123
Plan the project	0.118	0.238**	0.147	0.178*	0.112	0.108	0.096	0.110
Manage project transitions	0.106	0.171*	0.072	0.056	0.068	0.093	0.052	0.099
Plan and facilitate change	0.008	0.235**	0.079	0.167*	0.047	-0.004	0.184*	0.039
Ensure business integration	0.031	0.250**	0.136	0.190*	0.051	0.012	0.224**	0.073
Prepare users	0.053	0.199*	0.006	0.130	0.082	0.060	0.218**	0.164
Communicate change	0.075	0.239**	0.140	0.160	0.090	0.084	0.152	0.054
Evaluate and improve performance	0.074	0.144	0.070	0.194*	0.147	0.079	0.215*	0.185*
Demonstrate self-awareness	0.236**	0.295**	0.115	0.119	0.230**	0.166	0.086	0.233**
Realize benefits	0.094	0.166	0.111	0.081	0.058	0.137	0.154	0.100

** Correlation is significant at the 0.01 level (2-tailed).   * Correlation is significant at the 0.05 level (2-tailed).

with overall project complexity is consistent with results from research that links requirements for emotional intelligence (EQ), of which self-awareness and self-management are components, with increasing levels of different types of project complexity (Müller, Geraldi, & Turner, 2012).

Considering the seven component dimensions of project complexity, strategic importance is significantly positively related with the widest range of practices, suggesting that the more strategically important the project, the higher the level of both project management and change implementation practices likely to be applied. This is consistent with other research that indicates that the more strategically driven an organization, the wider the range of project management practices that will be applied (Crawford & Cooke-Davies, 2012). Financial impact and number of organizational interfaces demonstrate the least association with specific practices.

Overall, however, practices drawn from the change implementation toolkit and the combined project management/change implementation toolkit appear to be more associated with a wider range of dimensions of complexity than the pure project management practice sets. This result appears reasonable, as in many projects, much of the complexity will have been dealt with in the early initiation and definition phases, often prior to assignment of the project manager.

Role and Background of the Practitioner

Role

Investigation of variation in use of practices by those in project, program, and change roles is a central aspect of this research. Analysis of variance techniques (ANOVA) was used to answer the question:

> Does use of project, program, and change related practices vary according to **role**?

Results of this analysis, shown in Table 4-4, show very interesting results. The only significant differences at $P<0.05$ level in use of project management, program, and change practices by role are in three control agenda areas: **plan the project** ($P=0.043$), **monitor and control progress** ($P=0.026$), and **manage project transitions** ($P=0.042$), plus **communicate change** ($P=0.038$) and **realize benefits** ($P=0.008$). Post-hoc analysis using Fisher's least significant difference (LSD) test provides insight into the nature of the differences in use of practices by the different roles, and these results are summarized in Table 4-3.

Table 4-3. Nature of differences in use of practices by role

Practice Set	Significance	Nature of Difference
Plan the project	0.043	Average for program roles is significantly greater than the average for change roles
Monitor and control progress	0.026	Average for project and program roles is significantly greater than the average for change roles
Manage project transitions	0.042	Average for project and program roles is significantly greater than the average for change roles
Realize benefits	0.008	Average for program roles is significantly greater than the average for project roles
Communicate change	0.038	Average for program roles is significantly greater than the average for project roles

These results confirm the view that project managers exercise a control agenda (Buchanan, 1991). However, the results also suggest that, in practice, and contrary to expectation, given the narrowness of the project standards and the tendency to treat projects in isolation, those in project roles do not use process and transition re-lated practices significantly less than those in change roles. This supports the findings of Thomas and Buckle Henning (2007) that successful project managers use a much wider toolkit than is documented in *A Guide to the Project Management Body of Knowledge (PMBOK® Guide)*—Third Edition (PMI, 2004). On the other hand,

Table 4-4. Statistically significant differences between use of practices by role (ANOVA)

		Sum of Squares	df	Mean Square	F	Significance
Make informed decisions	Between groups	0.621	2	0.310	0.536	0.586
	Within groups	79.328	137	0.579		
	Total	**79.949**	**139**			
Build support	Between groups	0.158	2	0.079	0.147	0.863
	Within groups	73.804	137	0.539		
	Total	**73.962**	**139**			
Manage communications	Between groups	3.338	2	1.669	2.381	0.096
	Within groups	96.012	137	0.701		
	Total	**99.350**	**139**			
Engage stakeholders	Between groups	2.247	2	1.124	1.990	0.141
	Within groups	77.368	137	0.565		
	Total	**79.615**	**139**			
Monitor and control progress	Between groups	6.519	2	3.260	3.766	0.026
	Within groups	116.861	135	0.866		
	Total	**123.381**	**137**			
Plan the project	Between groups	5.537	2	2.768	3.219	0.043
	Within groups	117.836	137	0.860		
	Total	**123.373**	**139**			
Manage project transitions	Between groups	6.284	2	3.142	3.234	0.042
	Within groups	132.124	136	0.971		
	Total	**138.408**	**138**			
Plan and facilitate change	Between groups	3.055	2	1.527	1.155	0.318
	Within groups	181.135	137	1.322		
	Total	**184.190**	**139**			
Ensure business integration	Between groups	2.248	2	1.124	1.002	0.370
	Within groups	153.709	137	1.122		
	Total	**155.957**	**139**			
Prepare users	Between groups	6.649	2	3.325	2.408	0.094
	Within groups	189.122	137	1.380		
	Total	**195.771**	**139**			
Communicate change	Between groups	9.130	2	4.565	3.337	0.038
	Within groups	187.405	137	1.368		
	Total	**196.536**	**139**			
Evaluate and improve performance	Between groups	4.121	2	2.061	2.009	0.138
	Within groups	140.514	137	1.026		
	Total	**144.636**	**139**			
Demonstrate self-awareness	Between groups	1.232	2	0.616	.568	0.568
	Within groups	147.401	136	1.084		
	Total	**148.633**	**138**			
Realize benefits	Between groups	13.796	2	6.898	4.987	0.008
	Within groups	188.106	136	1.383		
	Total	**201.902**	**138**			

those in project and program roles use project planning, monitoring, and controlling and transition or life cycle management practices more than those in change roles. This result suggests some support the views of those in general management who see application of (traditional) project management approaches as having potential to influence more effective implementation of change (Whittington et al., 2006; Lehmann, 2010).

The role of the program manager in leading organizational change (Pellegrinelli, 1997) and in ensuring realization of benefits (ref. *Managing Successful Programmes* [OGC, 2007] and other program manager standards) is confirmed by these results. Notably, the only significant differences in the average for use of benefits realization and change communication practices are that they are used at a higher level by those in program roles than by those in project roles. There is no significant difference in the averages for use of these practices between program roles and change roles.

The results concerning use of practices by role raise questions concerning the involvement of the various roles relative to the degree of organizational and behavioral change. Analysis indicated that those in project roles are less likely to work on projects with higher degrees of organizational and behavioral change than those in change roles ($P=0.025$). This result supports the reasonable assumption that those project roles, and to a lesser extent program roles, work on projects (and programs) across a wide spectrum in terms of requirement for organizational and behavioral change, while those in change roles are primarily involved in projects and programs involving higher degrees of change.

Age and Gender

A number of the research questions addressed in this study relate to the demographics and background of the practitioner. The first of these to be addressed is:

> Does use of project, program, and change related practices vary between practitioners according to **age**?

Using the three categories for age presented in Table 3-12 and the mean scores for use of project, program, and change practices presented in Table 3-5, analysis of variance techniques (ANOVA) found no significant differences in use of any of the practices at $P<0.05$ level. There is a trend, however, towards higher levels of use of all practices in the older age groups, which is consistent with assumption of more senior positions.

As we have only two values in this study for the independent variable, gender, an independent samples T-Test was chosen to find an answer to the following question:

> Does use of project, program, and change related practices vary between practitioners according to **gender**?

Using the variable for gender (Table 3-12) and the mean scores for use of project, program, and change practices presented in Table 3-5, an independent samples T-Test revealed no significant differences between the averages for use of practices on projects for males and females. Although not statistically significant, there is a general trend towards slightly higher averages for use of project management practices for males and for change implementation, project/change implementation, and program management practices for females.

Educational Background

Does use of project, program, and change related practices vary between practitioners with different **educational backgrounds**? To answer this question, analysis of variance techniques (ANOVA) was applied. Using the variable for highest level of qualification, which includes both academic qualifications and professional certifications (Table 3-15), and the mean scores for use of project, program, and change practices presented in Table 3-5, analysis of variance techniques (ANOVA) (Table 4-5) indicates significant differences in use of practices at $P<0.05$ level were found only for ensure business integration ($P=0.008$) and for evaluate and improve performance (0.002).

For both sets of practices, the key differentiator appears to be a project management certification. Those who hold a project management certification in addition to an undergraduate degree are more likely to use ensure business integration practices than those with only an undergraduate degree. For evaluation and improvement of project performance, a project management certification alone, or in combination with any of the levels of academic qualification, is associated with higher levels of use of the practices. This is an interesting finding given that neither the need to ensure business integration nor to evaluate and improve project performance are practices highlighted in the majority of standards upon which project management professional certifications are based.

Experience

Respondents were asked to provide information about their experience in either project management or change management or both. This information was requested to assist in answering the question:

> Does use of project, program, and change related practices vary between practitioners according to length and type of **experience**?

As described in the previous chapter, nearly all respondents (92 percent) claim some experience in project management, and a majority of respondents (65 percent) claim to have experience in change management. The average experience in project

Table 4-5. Statistically significant differences between use of practices by highest level of qualification (ANOVA)

		Sum of Squares	df	Mean Square	F	Significance
Make informed decisions	Between groups	2.208	5	0.442	0.761	0.579
	Within groups	77.741	134	0.580		
	Total	**79.949**	**139**			
Build support	Between groups	0.726	5	0.145	0.266	0.931
	Within groups	73.236	134	0.547		
	Total	**73.962**	**139**			
Manage communications	Between groups	3.698	5	0.740	1.036	0.399
	Within groups	95.652	134	0.714		
	Total	**99.350**	**139**			
Engage stakeholders	Between groups	4.876	5	0.975	1.748	0.128
	Within groups	74.740	134	0.558		
	Total	**79.615**	**139**			
Monitor and control progress	Between groups	6.506	5	1.301	1.470	0.204
	Within groups	116.875	132	0.885		
	Total	**123.381**	**137**			
Plan the project	Between groups	6.507	5	1.301	1.492	0.196
	Within groups	116.866	134	0.872		
	Total	**123.373**	**139**			
Manage project transitions	Between groups	9.345	5	1.869	1.926	0.094
	Within groups	129.063	133	0.970		
	Total	**138.408**	**138**			
Plan and facilitate change	Between groups	8.916	5	1.783	1.363	0.242
	Within groups	175.274	134	1.308		
	Total	**184.190**	**139**			
Ensure business integration	Between groups	16.996	5	3.399	3.278	0.008
	Within groups	138.961	134	1.037		
	Total	**155.957**	**139**			
Prepare users	Between groups	8.070	5	1.614	1.152	0.336
	Within groups	187.702	134	1.401		
	Total	**195.771**	**139**			
Communicate change	Between groups	12.956	5	2.591	1.891	0.100
	Within groups	183.579	134	1.370		
	Total	**196.536**	**139**			
Evaluate and improve performance	Between groups	19.124	5	3.825	4.083	0.002
	Within groups	125.512	134	0.937		
	Total	**144.636**	**139**			
Demonstrate self-awareness	Between groups	4.865	5	0.973	0.900	0.483
	Within groups	143.768	133	1.081		
	Total	**148.633**	**138**			
Realize benefits	Between groups	9.058	5	1.812	1.249	0.290
	Within groups	192.844	133	1.450		
	Total	**201.902**	**138**			

management is 10 years, and the average for change management is just under half of this. Participants have experience in either project management or change implementation or experience in both (see Table 3-17).

Using the variable that details project and change management experience (Table 3-17) and the mean scores for use of project, program, and change practices presented in Table 3-5, analysis of variance techniques (ANOVA) (Table 4-7) indicates significant differences in use of practices at $P<0.05$ level only for engage stakeholders ($P=0.042$), monitor and control progress ($P<0.001$), plan the project ($P<0.001$), manage project transitions ($P=0.10$), and evaluate and improve performance ($P=0.036$). It is not surprising that practices are used at significantly higher levels by those who have either project management experience or both project and change implementation experience. Overall, however, for these practices that are used at significantly higher levels, project management experience is the key differentiator.

To determine whether use of practices varies according to the number of years of experience, a correlation analysis of use of the practices (dependent variables) and the independent variables, project management experience (years) and change implementation (years), was undertaken. The results of this analysis (see Table 4-6),

Table 4-6. Pearson correlations between use of practices and number of years' experience in either project management or change implementation

Practices	Project Management Experience (Years)	Change Implementation Experience (Years)
Make informed decisions	0.204*	0.152
Build support	0.154	0.152
Manage communications	0.284**	0.193*
Engage stakeholders	0.264**	0.224**
Monitor and control progress	0.290**	0.152
Plan the project	0.236**	0.167*
Manage project transitions	0.199*	0.126
Plan and facilitate change	0.228**	0.250**
Ensure business integration	0.162*	0.156
Prepare users	0.193*	0.145
Communicate change	0.236**	0.271**
Evaluate and improve performance	0.301**	0.166*
Demonstrate self-awareness	0.108	0.149
Realize benefits	0.150	0.054

** Correlation is significant at the 0.01 level (2-tailed).   * Correlation is significant at the 0.05 level (2-tailed).

show strong correlations between the number of years of experience and use of practices. Number of years of **project management experience** is most strongly correlated at (P<0.01) with half of the sets of practices, primarily those that are based in project management standards but notably including plan and facilitate change and communicate change. One might speculate that this result reflects an interpretation of change in the sense of change control. However, as can be seen from the individual items that comprise these sets of practices (Appendix E), it may be considered more likely that experienced practitioners have learned, from experience, the value and importance of such practices to successful outcomes. Understandably, the practices with strongest correlations (P<0.01) with increasing number of years of experience in **change implementation practices** are directly change related: engage stakeholders, plan and facilitate change, and communicate change.

Clearly, use of project, program, and change related practices varies between practitioners according to length and type of experience. Project management experience is the strongest differentiator. The more years of project management experience, the more likely the practitioner is to use the practices at a higher level. The same is true for change implementation practices. Those with more years of change management experience, remembering that the average is five years, which is half the average for project management experience, the more likely the practitioner is to use the practices at a higher level.

Underpinning Knowledge

As discussed in the literature review, the fields of project management and change implementation are founded in different bodies of knowledge. Traditional project management draws largely upon operations research and systems engineering, while change implementation is based in disciplines of organizational behavior and development. Underpinning knowledge and understanding are considered important aspects of competence, yet research has indicated that practices are often more generic than knowledge (Crawford & Pollack, 2007). Practitioners may use similar practices, although they may be operating from different conceptualizations and knowledge bases. The research question to be answered by this analysis is therefore:

> Is there a difference in levels of underpinning project management and change implementation **knowledge** between roles?

As explained in the previous chapter, respondents were asked to complete brief tests of key concepts in project management and change implementation to provide an overall indicator of level of knowledge in each field. Using the variables for project management knowledge and change implementation knowledge (Table 3-19) and the variable representing project, program, and change roles (Table 3-11), analysis of

Table 4-7. Statistically significant differences between use of practices by experience (ANOVA)

ANOVA

		Sum of Squares	df	Mean Square	F	Significance
Make informed decisions	Between groups	2.800	3	0.933	1.645	0.182
	Within groups	77.149	136	0.567		
	Total	**79.949**	**139**			
Build support	Between groups	1.209	3	0.403	0.753	0.522
	Within groups	72.753	136	0.535		
	Total	**73.962**	**139**			
Manage communications	Between groups	1.362	3	0.454	0.630	0.597
	Within groups	97.987	136	0.720		
	Total	**99.350**	**139**			
Engage stakeholders	Between groups	4.647	3	1.549	2.810	0.042
	Within groups	74.968	136	0.551		
	Total	**79.615**	**139**			
Monitor and control progress	Between groups	15.676	3	5.225	6.501	0.000
	Within groups	107.705	134	0.804		
	Total	**123.381**	**137**			
Plan the project	Between groups	18.991	3	6.330	8.248	0.000
	Within groups	104.382	136	0.768		
	Total	**123.373**	**139**			
Manage project transitions	Between groups	11.142	3	3.714	3.940	0.010
	Within groups	127.266	135	0.943		
	Total	**138.408**	**138**			
Plan and facilitate change	Between groups	4.345	3	1.448	1.095	0.353
	Within groups	179.845	136	1.322		
	Total	**184.190**	**139**			
Ensure business integration	Between groups	3.475	3	1.158	1.033	0.380
	Within groups	152.482	136	1.121		
	Total	**155.957**	**139**			
Prepare users	Between groups	1.788	3	0.596	0.418	0.741
	Within groups	193.984	136	1.426		
	Total	**195.771**	**139**			
Communicate change	Between groups	6.328	3	2.109	1.508	0.215
	Within groups	190.208	136	1.399		
	Total	**196.536**	**139**			
Evaluate and improve performance	Between groups	8.756	3	2.919	2.921	0.036
	Within groups	135.880	136	0.999		
	Total	**144.636**	**139**			
Demonstrate self-awareness	Between groups	0.302	3	0.101	0.091	0.965
	Within groups	148.332	135	1.099		
	Total	**148.633**	**138**			
Realize benefits	Between groups	2.424	3	0.808	0.547	0.651
	Within groups	199.478	135	1.478		
	Total	**201.902**	**138**			

variance techniques (ANOVA) (Table 4-8) confirms that there are significant differences at P<0.05 level in underpinning change implementation knowledge between roles. There is no significant difference in project management knowledge between the roles. As might be expected, change implementation knowledge is significantly greater for those in change roles than for those in project roles (P=0.007).

Table 4-8. Statistically significant differences between underpinning project and change implementation knowledge by role (ANOVA)

ANOVA

		Sum of Squares	df	Mean Square	F	Significance
Project management knowledge	Between groups	14.919	2	7.459	1.013	0.366
	Within groups	993.690	135	7.361		
	Total	**1008.609**	**137**			
Change implementation knowledge	Between groups	54.974	2	27.487	4.042	0.020
	Within groups	918.019	135	6.800		
	Total	**972.993**	**137**			

No significant correlations (P<0.05) were found between underpinning project management or change implementation knowledge and use of any of the practices in Table 3-5. This may be seen as further support for the generic nature of practices relative to the more contextually driven nature of project management knowledge (Crawford & Pollack, 2007).

Likelihood of Project Success

The final question posed in this research is:

> Can use of any project, program, and change related practices be identified
> as predictors of perceived likelihood of **project success**?

The primary analytical approach to answering this question is exploratory, but there is one important underlying assumption that lends itself to confirmatory analysis. As stated previously, the project management, change implementation, and benefits realization practices included in the analysis have been drawn from standards documents developed by practitioners. It may therefore be assumed that all the practices will be significantly correlated to project success.

To test the hypothesis that all project management, change implementation, and benefits realization practices are significantly correlated to overall project success, a correlation analysis of the practices (independent variables) (Table 3-5) and the dependent variable, overall project success (Table 3-21), and its four components (time performance, budget performance, stakeholder satisfaction, and benefits delivery [Table 3-20]) was conducted.

As shown in Table 4-9, all practice variables were significantly positively related ($P<=0.05$) with overall project success, confirming this hypothesis. All but one practice variable, demonstrate self-awareness, were correlated with a significance level of $P<=0.01$. Demonstrate self-awareness was the only practice variable that was only significantly correlated with overall project success and not with any of its components.

Table 4-9. Pearson correlations between success criteria and use of practices

	Overall Project Success	Stakeholder Satisfaction	Time Performance	Budget Performance	Benefits Delivery
Make informed decisions	0.453**	0.297**	0.287**	0.284**	0.320**
Build support	0.237**	0.127	0.181*	0.123	0.121
Manage communications	0.296**	0.133	0.176*	0.232**	0.155
Engage stakeholders	0.289**	0.180*	0.155	0.244**	0.153
Monitor and control progress	0.243**	0.228**	0.081	0.150	0.113
Plan the project	0.250**	0.215*	0.169*	0.156	0.096
Manage project transitions	0.300**	0.236**	0.178*	0.197*	0.201*
Plan and facilitate change	0.373**	0.204*	0.280**	0.351**	0.229**
Ensure business integration	0.378**	0.268**	0.290**	0.316**	0.289**
Prepare users	0.319**	0.197*	0.150	0.322**	0.234**
Communicate change	0.312**	0.184*	0.197*	0.303**	0.202*
Evaluate and improve performance	0.308**	0.179*	0.203*	0.291**	0.146
Demonstrate self-awareness	0.184*	0.102	0.092	0.107	0.130
Realize benefits	0.244**	0.189*	0.129	0.216*	0.160

** Correlation is significant at the 0.01 level (2-tailed).   * Correlation is significant at the 0.05 level (2-tailed).   Shaded cells are NOT significantly correlated.

Make informed decisions and ensure business integration are significantly correlated with overall project success and all four of its components at $P=0.01$. Manage project transitions, plan and facilitate change, and communicate change are significantly correlated with overall project success and all four of its components at either $P=0.01$ or $P<0.05$.

A correlation analysis (Table 4-10) was also conducted between perceived likelihood of project success and eight contextual factors. These were the seven dimensions of management complexity (Table 3-10) and degree of organizational and behavioral change (Table 3-7).

Table 4-10. Pearson correlations between success criteria and contextual factors

	Overall Project Success	Stakeholder Satisfaction	Time Performance	Budget Performance	Benefits Delivery
Stability of context	0.430**	0.191*	0.304**	0.373**	0.259**
Number of disciplines and methods	0.140	0.216*	0.009	-0.025	0.158
Legal, social, environmental implications	0.022	0.088	-0.092	-0.123	0.092
Financial impact	0.053	0.075	-0.076	-0.179*	0.223**
Strategic importance	0.263**	0.212*	0.079	0.042	0.221**
Stakeholder cohesion	0.391**	0.255**	0.315**	0.146	0.212*
Organizational interfaces	0.149	0.176*	0.061	-0.072	0.136
Degree of organizational and behavioral change	0.053	0.067	-0.040	-0.011	-0.028

** Correlation is significant at the 0.01 level (2-tailed).   * Correlation is significant at the 0.05 level (2-tailed).   Shaded cells are NOT significantly correlated.

Only stability of context, strategic importance, and stakeholder cohesion showed significant correlation with overall project success. In other words, the more stable the context, the more strategically important the project, and the more cohesive the stakeholders, the higher the likelihood of overall project success. Stability of context was the only contextual factor that showed significant correlation not only with overall success but with all of its four components. It is not surprising that an increasing number of disciplines, methods, and organizational interfaces are likely to impact stakeholder satisfaction. The relationship between financial impact and budget performance and between financial impact and benefits delivery also has face validity. Notably, there was no significant correlation between degree of organizational and behavioral change and any of the dimensions of project success.

Analysis of variance techniques (ANOVA) was then applied to check whether the mean score for overall project success is significantly different for each of the eight project characteristics. Results confirmed that there are significant differences (at $P < 0.01$ level) in mean scores for overall project success relative to stability of context ($P = 0.001$) and stakeholder cohesion ($P = 0.001$). This analysis also highlighted a significant difference (at $P < 0.05$) level relative to strategic importance ($P = 0.021$). No significant differences were revealed for the remaining five project characteristics, including degree of organizational and behavioral change. This confirms stability of context, stakeholder cohesion, and strategic importance as key factors that are likely to have impact on the success of projects.

To investigate the influence of the remaining contextual variables, public private sector and industry sector, and internal or external clients, independent samples T-Tests were used to determine if the mean of overall project success and its components is the same for both parts of the sample.

Results for the public vs. private sector indicated a significant difference in the mean for overall project success (P=0.033) and for stakeholder satisfaction (P=0.037). The difference indicates that success rates are higher for the private sector than for the public sector.

For the industry sectors, no significant difference was found between results for the finance and services sector and the engineering sector.

The only significant difference in the means of overall success and its components for internal and external clients is in benefits delivery, where the means are higher, and therefore the performance better, for projects carried out for external rather than internal clients (P=0.029).

To explore the relationship between project management and change implementation practices and project success, the selected approach is logistic regression. This form of analysis is well suited to identification of critical success factors, as the goal is to correctly predict the category of outcome for individual cases using the most parsimonious model. To accomplish this goal, a model is created that includes all independent variables that are useful in predicting the response variable.

Logistic regression requires a binary or dichotomous dependent variable. As we are aiming to distinguish factors critical to the success of projects, it is beneficial to provide a clear split between those projects likely to be considered successful and those likely to be considered unsuccessful. Using the values for overall likelihood of project success, as presented in Table 3-21, we can identify three groups, with low, medium, and high likelihood of project success. Removal from analysis of the 16 cases in the medium category (Table 3-21), which also happens to be the median, not only provides us with a useful binary dependent variable but also slightly increases the reliability from $\alpha=0.774$ to $\alpha=0.798$ with minimal loss of data (n=124).

Using the logistic regression approach, a series of models were fitted using only the high and low values of the dependent or predictor variable *overall likelihood of project success* with low or high values and selected independent variables (*project management, change implementation, and benefits realization practices, project characteristics*). This approach was used to find models that would best predict the probability of being in either group (low likelihood or high likelihood of project success) for a given set of explanatory variables. As the previous correlation analysis (Tables 4-9 and 4-10) has shown, most of these variables by themselves are significantly correlated to overall project success, so many predictive logistic regression models are possible. In the interests of parsimony and in order to identify the smallest number of practices and contextual factors, a backwards logistic regression was used to determine which of the 22 variables are of greater assistance in predicting the overall likelihood of project success. Results of this analysis are shown in Table 4-11.

Table 4-11. Logistic regression model for predicting overall likelihood of project success

Variables Entered in the First Equation	Coefficients in Equation with All Variables Included (74.1% Correct Classification)	Coefficients in Final Equation with Nonsignificant Variables Excluded (73.3% Correct Classification)
PRACTICES		
Make informed decisions	0.893	0.743
Build support	0.388	
Manage communications	0.219	
Engage stakeholders	-1.546	
Monitor and control progress	-0.277	
Plan the project	0.296	
Manage project transitions	0.043	
Plan and facilitate change	-0.162	
Ensure business integration	1.019	0.593
Prepare users	0.398	
Communicate change	0.411	
Evaluate and improve performance	0.190	
Demonstrate self-awareness	-0.520	
Realize benefits	-0.380	
CONTEXTUAL VARIABLES		
Stability of context	1.174	0.767
Number of disciplines and methods	0.452	
Legal, social, environmental implications	-0.579	
Financial impact	-0.478	
Strategic importance	1.071	
Stakeholder cohesion	0.540	0.874
Organizational interfaces	0.409	
Degree of organizational and behavioral change	-0.189	
Constant	-10.619	-8.931

The initial logistic regression model with all 22 variables included correctly classified 74.1 percent of the 124 cases in the analysis.

The final and most parsimonious logistic regression model identified four variables that correctly classified 73.3 percent of the 124 people in the dataset. These four variables, which can be considered statistically significant critical success factors are:

Practices: Make informed decisions, ensure business integration

Contextual Variables: Stability of context and stakeholder cohesion

The full model, including project management, change implementation, and benefits realization practices, correctly classified 74.1 percent of the sample. However, the more parsimonious models include only practices from the change implementation toolset. By looking beyond the traditional project management tools, techniques, and practices in search of other factors that influence the likelihood of project success, the results demonstrate that change implementation practices are more significant predictors of project success than project management practices, regardless of industry sector and degree of organizational and behavioral change. This result is consistent with Lechler and Byrne's (2010) findings concerning the value mindset for project managers and the impact of entrepreneurial practices on the success of projects.

The results of this research confirm the association of use of project management practices with the success of projects. However, by looking beyond the traditional project management tools, techniques, and practices in search of other factors that influence the likelihood of project success, the results demonstrate that the practices identified as most critical to project success are those drawn from the change implementation toolkit, namely make informed decisions and ensure business integration.

It is particularly interesting that higher levels of use of practices associated with engagement of stakeholders as associated with decreasing odds of achieving project success. This can be read in conjunction with the two contextual variables that are identified as critical success factors, stability of context and stakeholder cohesion. Where the project context is stable and there is a high level of agreement and cohesion among stakeholders, the project is more likely to be successful. A project operating in this environment is not only more likely to be successful but is less likely to need a high level of stakeholder engagement activity than one that is subject to high levels of contextual instability and disagreement among stakeholders. High levels of stakeholder engagement may therefore be associated with projects that are inherently more difficult and therefore less likely to be successful.

Chapter 5

Conclusions

All change initiatives can be considered projects or programs, and the majority of projects involve some degree of organizational and behavioral change. The degree of this change can be expected to be greater in projects where the purpose is to achieve organizational change, but even where the focus is on other outcomes, achievement of desired benefits may require structural changes and will generally involve some change in the way people do things.

This intersection of change and project management is attracting interest from both practitioners and researchers because, in a rapidly changing and evolving environment, an organization's ability to change itself has become critical to strategic performance. Much of the responsibility for organizational change rests in the hands of general management, but devolution of parts of this responsibility to specific change management roles is occurring and there is widespread acceptance of projects and programs as organizing frameworks for change initiatives. However, the fields of project and change management rest on different foundations and have developed in different directions. Although project and program managers claim to be implementers of change, literature review and qualitative research (Crawford & Hassner-Nahmias, 2010) suggest that current professional standards and certification in project management do not require them to have the full range of competencies required to effectively manage change.

To provide insight into the reality of practice on projects involving varying degrees of organizational and behavioral change, this research report presents results of a quantitative study designed to identify:

- The nature of project, program, and change related practices associated with the management of projects;
- Potential variation in use of project, program, and change related practices according to the nature of the project, including:
  o industry sector
  o client—internal or external to the performing organization
  o degree of management complexity
  o degree of organizational change involved;
- The practitioner role and background; and

- The relative contribution of use of project, program, and change implementation practices to likelihood of project success.

Study respondents were asked to describe and provide an assessment of the likelihood of success of two of their most recent projects. They were then asked to identify the level at which they had used, on these projects, a number of project, program, and change implementation practices. Additionally, they provided demographic and background data on experience and qualifications and completed a brief test to assess their underpinning knowledge of project management and organizational change.

Summary of Key Results

Nature and Use of Project Management and Change Implementation Practices

Overall level of use of all practices is high (mean scores of 2.92 to 3.78 with a maximum of 5). The four most highly used sets of practices across this sample involve engagement with others in order to achieve results: making informed decisions, building support, managing communications, and engaging stakeholders. These are followed by those practices that are central to current standards for management of projects, namely, planning, monitoring and controlling, and managing across the project life cycle (manage project transitions) with mean scores from 3.29 to 3.50. Next come four sets of practices that may be considered central to the change implementation toolkit: planning and facilitating change, communicating change, preparing users, and ensuring integration with the business.

In keeping with a number of other studies, notably Crawford and Cooke-Davies (2012), the least used practices are those associated with realization of benefits. Although benefits realization is a hot topic among practitioners at all levels, and many organizations now require benefits to be identified when approving business cases for projects, action to ensure that these benefits are realized is less common. A number of factors contribute to this. First, there is the argument that the project manager is responsible for outputs and the program manager or general management are responsible for delivery of outcomes or benefits from the project. This view is firmly ingrained in the OGC (now U.K. Cabinet Office) suite of standards for management of projects, including PRINCE2 and *Managing Successful Programmes* (MSP). However, for the subset of program managers in the sample reported here, benefits realization practices is still among those reported to be least used. Implementation of practices to ensure delivery of benefits appears to be among the greatest challenges still facing organizations in terms of achieving value from their projects. This study reinforces this view.

In summary, although over 50 percent of the sample in this study are in project roles, the most highly used practices across all project roles and types are drawn from the change implementation or organizational change toolkit.

Nature of the Project

Having investigated the overall level of use of project, program, and change implementation practices, the next step was to see whether there were any significant variations in use of practices according to the nature of the project and its context.

Degree of Organizational and Behavioral Change

There is clear evidence of variation in use of project, program, and change practices relative to the degree of organizational and behavioral change of projects. As might be expected, change implementation practices (make informed decisions, build support, prepare users, and communicate change) and practices common to both change implementation and project management (engage stakeholders and manage communications) are used at higher levels on projects requiring higher degrees of organizational and behavioral change.

Of equal interest, however, are those practices where there is clearly no evidence of significant difference relative to degree of organizational and behavioral change. It is not surprising that there is no significant variation in use of project management and control agenda practices (monitor and control progress, manage project transitions, evaluate and improve performance, realize benefits) on projects requiring differing levels of organizational and behavioral change. Benefits realization is the least used set of practices overall, demonstration of self-awareness may be considered a generic practice, and project management is expected to be a part of the change manager's toolkit (Change Management Institute, 2008). However, planning and facilitating change and ensuring business integration are drawn entirely from the change implementation toolkit, so it might have been expected that they would have been used at a higher level on projects requiring higher degrees of organizational and behavioral change. This is not the case. It appears that practices involved in preparing the people and the organization for change and ensuring that the product of the project is integrated with ongoing business operations are used largely independent of the degree of organizational and behavioral change required.

Sector

Public vs. Private Sector

All project, program, and change implementation practices are used at significantly higher levels in the private sector than in the public sector, with the exception of building support.

Notably, building support is one of the most highly used sets of practices and, although drawn from the change implementation toolkit, may be considered an activity that would be common to all management roles. This finding that project management practices are used at a higher level in the private sector relative to the public sector is consistent with other contemporaneous studies (Crawford & Cooke-Davies, 2012).

Industry Sector

Two broad industry sectors are represented in this study: finance and business services, and engineering and construction. Across these two sectors, there is no significant variation in use of project management practices, or the more generic change implementation practices. Benefits realization, and four sets of specific change implementation practices (plan and facilitate change, ensure business integration, prepare users, and communicate change), are used at significantly higher levels in the finance and business services sector than in engineering and construction. The significantly higher use of benefits realization practices in the finance and business services sector is consistent with results from other studies indicating a higher number of projects with intangible rather than tangible outcomes in this sector (Crawford & Cooke-Davies, 2012).

Client

The only significant differences in use of practices on projects for internal and external clients are in making informed decisions and monitoring and controlling progress, which are used at a higher level on projects for external clients than for internal clients. This result, plus a non-significant but general trend for all practices to be used at higher levels on projects for external clients, may be seen as consistent with circumstances associated with such projects, which may include contract conditions and desire for repeat business.

Management Complexity

As complexity is a composite attribute (Crawford et al., 2006), seven dimensions of complexity were investigated: strategic importance; number of organizational interfaces; stakeholder cohesion; number of disciplines and methods; financial impact; stability of context; and legal, social, and environmental implications. The means of these seven dimensions were combined to provide a mean score for overall project success.

Three sets of practice variables were found to be significantly positively correlated ($P <= 0.05$) with overall project complexity: building support, managing communications, and demonstrating self-awareness.

Practices drawn from the change implementation toolkit, and the combined project management/change implementation toolkit appear to be more associated with a wider range of dimensions of complexity than the pure project management practice sets. This is consistent with the execution focus of the traditional project management toolkit (Morris, Crawford, Hodgson, Shepherd, & Thomas, 2006), which was designed to deal with projects where most of the complexity had been dealt with through the proposal process. This finding in particular supports results from earlier research calling for an expansion of the coverage and concept of project management (Winter et al., 2006; Sahlin-Andersson & Söderholm, 2002; Cicmil et al., 2006) in terms of what might therefore be included in standards. Addition of change tools and techniques to project management standards would provide additional support for practitioners in dealing with complex and not just simple projects.

Of the seven component dimensions of project complexity, strategic importance is significantly positively related with the widest range of practices, suggesting that the more strategically important the project, the higher the level of both project management and change implementation practices likely to be applied.

Role and Background of the Practitioner

Role

It may be expected that those in project and program roles will be involved in a wide range of project types with varying degrees of organizational and behavioral change, while those in change roles are most likely to be involved where there is expectation that more, rather than less, change needs to be implemented. It is therefore not surprising that those in project roles are less likely to work on projects with higher degrees of organizational and behavioral change than those in change roles (P=0.025).

A particularly interesting finding of this study is that the only significant differences in use of project, program, and change related practices by those in project and change implementation roles is that those in project roles are more likely to use higher levels of three sets of control agenda practices drawn from the project management toolkit: planning the project, monitoring and controlling progress, and managing project transitions. The flip side of this finding is that there is no significant difference between use of the process agenda practices, drawn from the change implementation toolkit, between those in project and change roles. This suggests that although standards for project management focus on a control agenda and are largely silent on practices related to implementation of desirable change, project management practitioners, in the workplace, are utilizing a much wider practice set that encompasses change implementation.

A further finding is that those in program roles are using benefits realization and change communication practices at higher levels than those in project roles. This finding is consistent with definitions of program management roles promulgated in guides such as *Managing Successful Programmes* (U.K. Cabinet Office, 2011).

Age and Gender

Our data revealed no significant differences between the averages for use of practices on projects according to age or gender.

Educational Background

Significant difference in use of practices at P<0.05 level, relative to educational background, were found only for ensure business integration (P=0.008) and for evaluate and improve performance (0.002). For both sets of practices, the key differentiator appears to be a project management certification.

Experience

Nearly all respondents (92 percent) claim some experience in project management, and a majority of respondents (65 percent) claim to have experience in change management. The average experience in project management is 10 years, and the average for change management is just under half of this.

The number of years of project management experience is most strongly correlated at ($P<0.01$) with half of the sets of practices, primarily those that are based in project management standards but notably including plan and facilitate change and communicate change. The practices with the strongest correlations ($P<0.01$) with increasing number of years of experience in change implementation practices are engaging stakeholders and planning, facilitating, and communicating change, all of which are directly change related.

Use of project, program, and change related practices varies between practitioners according to length and type of experience. Project management experience is the strongest differentiator. The more years of project management experience, the more likely the practitioner is to use the practices at a higher level. The same is true for change implementation practices. The more years of change management experience a practitioner has, remembering that the average is five years, which is half the average for project management experience, the more likely the practitioner is to use the practices at a higher level. This is consistent with an expectation that maturity and seniority will increase in line with experience.

Underpinning Knowledge

There is no significant difference in project management knowledge between the roles. As might be expected, change implementation knowledge is significantly greater for those in change roles than for those in project roles.

Likelihood of Project Success

The results of this research confirm the association of use of project management practices with the success of projects. However, by looking beyond the traditional project management tools, techniques, and practices in search of other factors that influence the likelihood of project success, the results demonstrate that the practices identified as most critical to project success are those drawn from the change implementation toolkit, namely making informed decisions and ensuring business integration.

It is particularly interesting that higher levels of use of practices associated with engagement of stakeholders are associated with decreasing odds of achieving project success. This can be read in conjunction with the two contextual variables that are identified as critical success factors, stability of context and stakeholder cohesion. Where the project context is stable and there is a high level of agreement and cohesion among stakeholders, the project is more likely to be successful. A project operating in this environment is not only more likely to be successful but is less likely to need a high level of stakeholder engagement activity than one that is subject to high levels of contextual instability and disagreement among stakeholders. High levels of stakeholder engagement may therefore be associated with projects that are inherently more difficult and therefore less likely to be successful.

Recommendations for Practice

From a project management perspective, a major finding of this research is that those in project roles appear to be embracing change implementation practices despite their absence from the main project management standards for both knowledge and performance. Project management practitioners are using change implementation practices across a range of projects requiring differing degrees of organizational and behavioral change, and across both the finance and engineering sectors.

Use of all project, program, and change implementation practices is associated with the success of projects, but to increase the likelihood of success, practitioners should place particular emphasis on making informed decisions and ensuring business integration. Those who hold some form of project management professional certification appear to be more likely to use higher levels of business integration practice.

Junior and entry-level project practitioners should take note that more experienced project managers are using practices from both the project management and change implementation toolkits. They should recognize that to be successful in their roles, they must use practices that go beyond the traditional project management tools and techniques presented in current project management standards.

Training, education, and development of project practitioners at all levels should go beyond the current project management standards and traditional toolset and encompass introduction and guidance in use of change implementation practices. This supports a current trend toward training and development in "soft skills."

From the perspective of those in general management leading change, there is evidence from this research that project and program managers do offer planning, monitoring, and control and life cycle management capabilities and that these capabilities are less likely to be provided by those in change roles. This should be considered when resourcing projects.

An implication of the ubiquity of use of change implementation practices and the importance of such practices to achievement of successful outcomes is that the change implementation dimension should be recognized in considering role descriptions for management of a wide range of projects, beyond those directly focused on organizational change.

Research-Based Suggestions for Additions to Project Management Standards

It is a widely accepted tenet of standards development that standards should generally be limited to recognition of practices in use and reflect those practices used by most project managers on most projects. This is particularly important for performance-based standards where assessment is based on provision of evidence of use in the workplace. A key finding of this research, with implications for standards development, is that change implementation practices are in use by practitioners and should therefore be recognized in project management standards. The change implementation practices identified in this study provide a useful starting point.

Concluding Remarks, Limitations, and Future Research

The foregoing recommendations are directed to a project management audience. Insights from this research have implications also for those whose primary interest is organizational change, specifically those in change manager and other change implementation roles. The findings from the research, for instance, may be of value to the Change Management Institute and other emerging professional associations in the change field as an input to further development of their own standards.

This area, between project and change management, is a grey area that is clearly evolving. In practice, there is often tension between project and change managers, and there is considerable confusion and lack of clarity concerning roles. While many experienced project managers take it for granted that planning for change and ensuring business integration are part of their role, there are others in project roles who either don't consider it or who consider it to be the responsibility of others. This latter view is reflected in current project management standards. The interface between projects and change implementation is clearly in a state of flux and has significant potential for further research and investigation.

Professional formation for change implementation is in its infancy, and one possibility or opportunity is for the project management profession, which is far more advanced in its development, to extend its coverage to incorporate change implementation. As the field of project management claims that projects bring about change and that project management is recognized as the most efficient way of managing such change (APM, 2006, p. 2), this could be a logical progression.

Given the implications of this research for the current and future practice of both project management and change implementation, and the potential for future research, it is important to identify the limitations of this study and provide some suggestions for future investigation.

A limitation of this study is the industry distribution and the sample size, especially in the light of analyses across three sets of roles: project, program, and change implementation. Over half the respondents are in project roles and less than

20 percent are in change roles. Future research with a larger sample, more evenly distributed across these three sets of roles, would provide an opportunity to test the results with a more balanced role distribution.

The industry distribution for this study covers finance and engineering. This is a good starting point because the two sectors can be seen as having different characteristics, especially in dealing with change. On the surface, from a practitioner perspective, the finance sector appears to be highly subject to business change and has been active in use of business analysts and change managers in this connection. It might be expected that the engineering sector would be less likely to have embraced a change implementation perspective, but discussion with people in the sector has identified the concept of operational readiness that is a concern for many engineering projects if they wish to deliver value. So the industry distribution, although limited to only two sectors, has been both interesting and informative. A larger, more diversified sample would, however, be useful in validating and supporting the generalizability of the results.

As with any study, the variables chosen for investigation are a limitation. For instance, when investigating the factors that contribute to the success of projects, the results will be limited by the variables or factors that are included in the investigation. Much of the research into project success factors has been limited to the traditional project management toolkit. In this study, the range of practices considered has been extended to include change implementation practices. There may, however, be other practices that are being used consistently by those in project, program, and/or change roles that have not yet been captured in documentation of project or change implementation skillsets. Qualitative research concerning the actuality of practice at the intersection between project and change implementation would be beneficial in gaining a better understanding of the field.

Having established to some extent the magnitude of the use of change implementation practices in project management, we now need to dig deeper to provide a richer understanding of what project, program, and change implementation practitioners do in practice through longitudinal observation-based studies.

Finally, it is important to note that among project managers, the term "change management" is problematic. When project managers use this term, they may be doing so in the sense of change control, or in the sense of implementing desirable change that is necessary to achieve project outcomes. This ambiguity of meaning should ideally be resolved. In this study, we have addressed this issue by adopting the term "change implementation" when referring to the organizational and behavioral change that needs to be implemented to achieve value from projects.

Appendix A

Human Research Ethics—
Explanatory Statement

Project Management and Organizational Change—
BUHREC Protocol Number: RO-970

Bond University, School of Sustainable Development, with support from the Project Management Institute, is undertaking research to enhance understanding of the relationship between project management and organizational change by investigating the project, program, and change related activities associated with organizational change projects and the extent to which such activities vary relative to the type of project/program, the context, and degree of organizational and behavioral change involved.

Our research approach is to ask project and change managers to complete a web-based questionnaire relating to their current project or change initiative and the change and project related activities in which they are engaged. The questionnaire also includes a brief knowledge test as an indicator of relative knowledge of project management, organizational change, and development concepts. The web-based questionnaire is designed to take no longer than 20-30 minutes to complete. We realize that this is a considerable time commitment, but the activity is designed to give useful feedback. Once individuals complete the questionnaire, we will send a report with individual project management and change management competency scores, explanatory text as to what each score means, and suggested development activities that can be undertaken to improve scores if you wish to do so.

The Bond University research team, for the purpose of research, will retain the data from these questionnaires in a format that does not identify you or your organization in any way, and those entrusted with handling the data have signed a statement of confidentiality as required by the Bond University Human Research Ethics Committee protocol for data handling.

Our intention is to use the research data gathered from this project as the basis for a research report and journal publications, but neither you nor your company will be identified in the publication except if a specific request is made, in which case you will have the opportunity to approve or deny publication of the text.

Your participation in this research is optional. Your management will not be informed if you wish to withdraw. Withdrawal can be for any or no reason at any time. No identifiable data will be shown to your management, and only you will receive a copy of your individual report.

This study has been approved by the Bond University Human Research Ethics Committee. If you have any complaints or reservations about any aspect of your participation in this research, you may contact the Ethics Committee through the Secretary, Caroline Carstens (phone: +61 7 559 54194; e-mail: buhrec@bond.edu.au). Any complaint you make will be treated in confidence and investigated fully, and you will be informed of the outcome.

Yours sincerely,

Lynn Crawford
Professor of Project Management
Bond University

Appendix B

Project Management Practices

These are the six units and 21 elements presented in the GAPPS Project Manager standards (GAPPS, 2007). These were used, without alteration, as a basis for data collection on project management practices.

Topic 1: Manage Stakeholder Relationships

1.1 Ensure that stakeholder interests are identified and addressed.

1.2 Promote effective individual and team performance.

1.3 Manage stakeholder communications.

1.4 Facilitate external stakeholder participation.

Topic 2: Manage Development of the Plan for the Project

2.1 Define the work of the project.

2.2 Ensure the plan for the project reflects relevant legal requirements.

2.3 Document risks and risk responses for the project.

2.4 Confirm project success criteria.

2.5 Develop and integrate project baselines.

Topic 3: Manage Project Progress

3.1 Monitor, evaluate, and control project performance.

3.2 Monitor risks to the project.

3.3 Reflect on practice.

Topic 4: Manage Product Acceptance

4.1 Ensure that the product of the project is defined.

4.2 Ensure that changes to the product of the project are monitored and controlled.

4.3 Secure acceptance of the product of the project.

Topic 5: Manage Project Transitions

5.1 Manage project start-up.

5.2 Manage transition between project phases.

5.3 Manage project closure.

Topic 6: Evaluate and Improve Project Performance

6.1 Develop a plan for project evaluation.

6.2 Evaluate the project in accordance with plan.

6.3 Capture and apply learning.

Appendix C

Change Implementation Practices (Original Set)

The Change Management Practitioner Competencies (Change Management Institute, 2008) propose 11 Skill Topic Areas (equivalent of Units) as shown below. Each Skill Topic Area has a number of associated indicative behaviors, which are similar to the elements in performance-based standards. In summary, there are 54 elements comprising a total of 147 statements.

1: Facilitating Change (5 elements, 16 statements)

The consideration of each change individually, and the planning of the most appropriate approach to the situation.

2: Strategic Thinking (4 elements, 12 statements)

The application of information on internal and external drivers for the change when scoping, planning, and making decisions.

3: Thinking and Judgment (3 elements, 11 statements)

The application of logic and thinking processes to analyze situations and problems so as to design effective solutions. The demonstration of the capacity to reflect, analyze, and develop workable frameworks and plans.

4: Influencing Others (4 elements, 11 statements)

The effective exploration of alternatives and positions so as to reach outcomes that gain all parties/support and acceptance.

5: Coaching for Change (6 elements, 9 statements)

The preparation of managers and employees for change through coaching in managing change skills, and the building of organization capability for the future.

6: Project Management (6 elements, 18 statements)

The application of knowledge, skills, tools, and techniques to project activities in order to meet or exceed stakeholder needs and expectations from the project.

7: Communication Skills (5 elements, 16 statements)

The building and maintaining of open, collaborative, and reciprocal relationships with others.

8: Self-Management (5 elements, 14 statements)

The assumption of full accountability for own performance in achieving change management outcomes.

9: Facilitation – Meetings and Workshops (4 elements, 16 statements)

The effective guidance of a group to appropriate and useful outcomes, in a constructive and timely manner.

10: Professional Development (3 elements, 7 statements)

A continual effort to gain more knowledge, develop more effective skills, and promote the profession of change management.

11: Specialist Expertise

The high level assessment of needs, approaches, design, and delivery methods for the implementation of solutions to meet business needs, incorporating:

Learning and Development (4 elements, 8 statements)

Communication (5 elements, 8 statements)

Appendix D

Change Implementation Practices (Revised Set)

For data collection purposes, the Change Management Practitioner Competencies (Change Management Institute, 2008) were reduced to 10 Skill Topic Areas/Units comprising a total of 42 elements as shown below. The content of the original standards was preserved as far as possible. The reduction in number of items for data collection was necessary to contain the time involved in completing the research instrument.

Review involved the following:

- Combining statement where possible where there was overlap or meaning.
- Removing original Skill Topic Area 6: Project Management, as this is covered by the Project Management Practices data collection instrument.
- Removing original Skill Topic Area 8: Self-Management, as this primarily contained personal behaviors rather than observable practices.
- Breaking Skill Topic Area 11: Specialist Expertise into its constituent parts to create Specialist Expertise: Learning and Development and Specialist Expertise: Communication.

The resulting 10 Skill Topic Areas/Units and 42 elements are shown below.

1: Facilitating Change (5 elements)

1.1 Apply the principles, behaviors, and skill of managing change.

1.2 Consider the organization's strategy, structure, process, and culture when diagnosing change.

1.3 Communicate and manage the business case for change.

1.4 Assess employees' readiness for the change and build communication plan.

1.5 Identify culture of the organization and design change plans accordingly.

2: Strategic Thinking (4 elements)

2.1 Identify the drivers for and scope of change in the organization.

2.2 Regularly monitor organizational readiness for change.

2.3 Identify likely impacts on business strategies and plans and alert business owners.

2.4 Build lasting solutions, owned by the business, that take account of other current and future changes in the business.

3: Thinking and Judgment (3 elements)

3.1 Work systematically to resolve problems, make informed decisions, and draw out key issues to identify underlying trends.

3.2 Maintain a holistic perspective, consider broad potential consequences of decisions, identify "root causes" of problems, and take appropriate action.

3.3 Set priorities, develop comprehensive solutions and plans, and make timely decisions.

4: Influencing Others (4 elements)

4.1 Identify stakeholders affected by the change and develop stakeholder engagement strategies.

4.2 Develop other people's confidence in your professional presence through consistent action and communication.

4.3 Form networks with other areas, industries, functions, and organizations that benefit the organization.

4.4 Modify own behavior in order to gain support for those ideas and plans from those in power.

5: Coaching for Change (5 elements)

5.1 Apply the principles of adult learning and coaching.

5.2 Identify the scope of change and prepare interventions, communication plans, and training accordingly.

5.3 Use coaching plans to increase overall organizational capability in managing change.

5.4 Act as a role model for others, share knowledge, and coach others.

5.5 Provide appropriate training and workplace learning opportunities that provide for the development of necessary new skills.

6: Project Management *(6 items, 18 statements) OMITTED (see previous note)*

6: Communication skills (5 elements)

6.1 Create and maintain value-added relationships by negotiating to achieve win/win outcomes in dealings with others, and supporting teamwork, rapport, and conflict resolution.

6.2 Use empathy to consider stakeholder views, plan stakeholder engagement, plan and prioritize activities, and tailor communication materials.

6.3 Adjust oral communication to the characteristics and needs of the audience, using open questions and active listening to ensure individuals/situations are clearly understood.

6.4 Express ideas clearly in documents that have organization, structure, grammar, language, and terminology adjusted to the characteristics and needs of the audience.

6.5 Regularly measure the effectiveness of communication and adjust approach accordingly, using the expertise of subject matter experts when designing communications and presentations.

8: Self Management (5 items, 14 statements) OMITTED (see previous note)

7: Facilitation – Meetings and Workshops (4 elements)

7.1 When designing a session, have a clear vision of its purpose and outcomes, and plan relevant group exercises, methods, and processes to deliver the desired outcomes.

7.2 Create and sustain a participatory environment by taking account of different styles, and provide opportunities for all group members to get involved.

7.3 Provide structure to meetings and workshops in terms of agenda, discussions, decision making, format, and environment.

7.4 Implement process by identifying issues and potential solutions, monitoring the event to ensure outcomes are met, taking action when a group member's behavior is impacting results, and bringing events to closure by summarizing actions and decisions.

8: Professional Development (3 elements)

8.1 Proactively seek out new and up-to-date information that can be applied to the change manager role, and assess and integrate that knowledge.

8.2 Seek feedback, focus skill development on under-developed areas, integrate new skills, and find opportunities to build new skills.

8.3 Provide simple explanations of the different aspects of change management to educate the business community.

9: Specialist Expertise: Learning and Development (4 elements)

9.1 Identify the learning and development needs of each audience group impacted by change, and apply adult learning principles.

9.2 Work with business owners and subject matter experts to ensure appropriate training plans are in place for all stakeholders.

9.3 Work with business owners to ensure implementation plans are in place for training rollouts to all impacted stakeholders, and monitor the rollout of that training.

9.4 Ensure results of training are evaluated, and provide reports to project manager and other stakeholders as required.

10: Specialist Expertise: Communication (5 elements)

10.1 Identify the communications needs of each stakeholder group impacted by change, in conjunction with business owners and subject matter experts.

10.2 Plan, document, and gain agreement to the approach to communication.

10.3 Work with key stakeholders to create most appropriate communications style, and utilize that style according to media and audience.

10.4 Monitor the development and delivery of communication solutions and report on progress to project manager.

10.5 Evaluate effectiveness, analyze the results of evaluation, and take required action.

Appendix E

Thematic Grouping of Units for Project, Program, and Change Practice

CONTROL AGENDA	Source	Ref. No.
Plan the Project		
Define the work of the project.	G	2.1
Ensure the plan for the project reflects relevant legal requirements.	G	2.2
Document risks and risk responses for the project.	G	2.3
Confirm project success criteria.	G	2.4
Develop and integrate project baselines.	G	2.5
Ensure that the product of the project is defined.	G	4.1
Monitor and Control Progress		
Monitor, evaluate, and control project performance.	G	3.1
Monitor risks to the project.	G	3.2
Ensure that changes to the product of the project are monitored and controlled.	G	4.2
Secure acceptance of the product of the project.	G	4.3
Manage Project Transitions		
Manage project start-up.	G	5.1
Manage transition between project phases.	G	5.2
Manage project closure.	G	5.3
Realize Benefits		
Design benefits and ensure ownership of benefits profile and benefits realization plan.	MSP	1.1
Implement projects that contribute to realizing expected benefits and outcomes.	MSP	1.2
Measure and communicate benefits accrual as projects deliver outcomes.	MSP	1.3

Initiate business assurance reviews to ensure capabilities are being embedded and established.	MSP	1.5
PROCESS AGENDA	**Source**	**Ref. No.**
Plan and Facilitate Change		
Apply the principles, behaviours and skill of managing change	C	1.1
Identify culture of the organisation and design change plans accordingly	C	1.5
Identify the drivers for and scope of change in the organisation	C	2.1
Regularly monitor organisational readiness for change	C	2.2
Build lasting solutions, owned by the business, which take account of other current and future changes in the business	C	2.4
Engage Stakeholders		
Identify stakeholders affected by the change and develop stakeholder engagement strategies	C	4.1
Use empathy to consider stakeholder views, plan stakeholder engagement, plan and prioritise activities and tailor communication materials	C	6.2
Create and sustain a participatory environment by taking account of different styles and provide opportunities for all group members to get involved	C	7.2
Work with business owners and subject matter experts to ensure appropriate training plans are in place for all stakeholders	C	9.2
Ensure that stakeholder interests are identified and addressed.	G	1.1
Manage stakeholder communications.	G	1.3
Facilitate external stakeholder participation.	G	1.4
Promote effective individual and team performance.	G	1.2
Manage communications		
Adjust oral communication to the characteristics and needs of the audience, using open questions and active listening to ensure individuals/situations are clearly understood	C	6.3
Express ideas clearly in documents which have organisation, structure, grammar, language and terminology adjusted to the characteristics and needs of the audience	C	6.4
Regularly measure the effectiveness of communication and adjust approach accordingly, using the expertise of subject matter experts when designing communications and presentations	C	6.5
When designing a session, have a clear vision of its purpose and outcomes, and plan relevant group exercises, methods and processes to deliver the desired outcomes	C	7.1
Provide structure to meetings and workshops in terms of agenda, discussions, decision making, format and environment	C	7.3
Implement process by identifying issues and potential solutions, monitoring the event to ensure outcomes are met, taking action when a group member's behaviour is impacting results, and bringing events to closure by summarising actions and decisions	C	7.4
Plan, document and gain agreement to the approach to communication	C	10.2
Work with key stakeholders to create most appropriate communications style, and utilise that style according to media and audience	C	10.3
Monitor the development and delivery of communication solutions and report on progress to project manager	C	10.4
Communicate change		
Assess employees' readiness for the change and build communication plan	C	1.4
Provide simple explanations of the different aspects of change management to educate the business community	C	8.3

Identify the communications needs of each stakeholder group impacted by change, in conjunction with business owners and subject matter experts	C	10.1

Prepare users

Apply the principles of adult learning and coaching	C	5.1
Identify the scope of change and prepare interventions, communication plans and training accordingly	C	5.2
Use coaching plans to increase overall organisational capability in managing change	C	5.3
Provide appropriate training and workplace learning opportunities that provide for the development of necessary new skills	C	5.5
Identify the learning and development needs of each audience group impacted by change, and apply adult learning principles	C	9.1
Work with business owners to ensure implementation plans are in place for training rollouts to all impacted stakeholders, and monitor the rollout of that training	C	9.3
Ensure results of training are evaluated and provide reports to project manager and other stakeholders as required	C	9.4

Build support

Develop other people's confidence in your professional presence through consistent action and communication	C	4.2
Form networks with other areas, industries, functions and organisations that benefit the organisation	C	4.3
Modify own behaviour in order to gain support for those ideas and plans from those in power	C	4.4
Create and maintain value added relationships by negotiating to achieve win/win outcomes in dealings with others, and supporting teamwork, rapport and conflict resolution	C	6.1

Ensure Business Integration

Consider the organisation's strategy, structure, process and culture when diagnosing change	C	1.2
Communicate and manage the business case for change	C	1.3
Assess progress, and monitor business stability and capability to cope with change.	MSP	1.4
Identify likely impacts on business strategies and plans and alert business owners	C	2.3

Make informed decisions

Work systematically to resolve problems, make informed decisions, and draw out key issues to identify underlying trends	C	3.1
Set priorities, develop comprehensive solutions and plans, and make timely decisions	C	3.3
Maintain a holistic perspective, consider broad potential consequences of decisions, identify 'root causes' to problems and take appropriate action	C	3.2

Demonstrate self-awareness

Act as a role model for others, share knowledge and coach others	C	5.4
Proactively seek out new and up-to-date information which can be applied to the change manager role, and assess and integrate that knowledge	C	8.1
Seek feedback, focus skill development on under developed areas, integrate new skills, and find opportunities to build new skills	C	8.2

Evaluate and improve performance

Capture and apply learning.	G	6.3
Reflect on practice.	G	3.3
Develop a plan for project evaluation.	G	6.1

Appendix F

Managerial Complexity Factors

Factor 1 - Stability of the Overall Project Context

General Descriptor

The project context includes the project life cycle, the stakeholders, the degree to which the applicable methods and approaches are known, and the wider socio-economic environment. When the project context is unstable—phase deliverables are poorly defined, scope changes are frequent and significant, team members are coming and going, applicable laws and regulations are being modified—the project management challenge increases. Aspects of "technical complexity," such as dealing with unproven concepts, would be considered here.

On the following four-point scale please rate the stability of the project context for each of the two projects you described.

Low Moderate High Very High

(values in database 4 3 2 1)

Factor 2 - Number of Distinct Disciplines, Methods, or Approaches Involved in Performing the Project

General Descriptor

Most projects involve more than one management or technical discipline; some projects involve a large number of different disciplines. For example, a project to develop a new drug could include medical researchers, marketing staff, manufacturing experts, lawyers, and others. Since each discipline tends to approach its part of the project in a different way, more disciplines mean a project that is relatively more difficult to manage.

Note: Some aspects of "technical complexity" such as dealing with a product with many interacting elements, would be considered here.

On the following four-point scale, please rate the number of distinct disciplines, methods, or approaches involved in performing each of the two projects you described.

Low Moderate High Very High

(values in database 1 2 3 4)

Factor 3 - Magnitude of Legal, Social, or Environmental Implications from Performing the Project

General Descriptor

This factor addresses the potential external impact of the project. For example, the potential for catastrophic failure means that the implications of constructing a nuclear power plant close to a major urban center will likely be much greater than those of constructing an identical plant in a remote area. The managerial complexity of the urban project will be higher due to the need to deal with a larger number of stakeholders and a more diverse stakeholder population.

On the following four-point scale, please rate the magnitude of legal, social, or environmental implications from performing each of the two projects you described.

Low Moderate High Very High

(values in database 1 2 3 4)

Factor 4 - Overall Expected Financial Impact (Positive or Negative) on the Project's Stakeholders

General Descriptor

This factor accounts for one aspect of the traditional measure of "size" but does so in relative terms. For example, a project manager in a consumer electronics start-up is subject to more scrutiny in terms of financial impact, than a project manager doing a similarly sized project for a computer manufacturer with operations around the globe.

Note: Where the impact on different stakeholders varies, this factor should be rated according to the impact on the primary stakeholders.

On the following four-point scale, please rate the overall expected financial impact (positive or negative) on the project's stakeholders for each of the two projects you described.

Low Moderate High Very High

(values in database 1 2 3 4)

Factor 5 - Strategic Importance of the Project

General Descriptor

This factor addresses yet another aspect of "size" and again deals with it in relative rather than absolute terms. While every project should be aligned with the organization's strategic direction, not every project can be of equal importance to the organization or organizations involved.

Note: As with financial impact, if the strategic importance for different stakeholders is different, this factor should be rated according to the strategic importance for the primary stakeholders.

On the following four-point scale, please rate the strategic importance of the project for each of the two projects you described.

Very Low Low Moderate High

(values in database 1 2 3 4)

Factor 6 - Stakeholder Cohesion Regarding the Characteristics of the Product of the Project

General Descriptor

When all or most stakeholders are in agreement about the characteristics of the product of the project, they tend to be in agreement about the expected outcomes as well. When they are not in agreement, or when the benefits of a product with a particular set of characteristics are unknown or uncertain, the project management challenge is significant.

On the following four-point scale, please rate the stakeholder cohesion regarding the characteristics of the product of the project for each of the two projects you described.

Very Low Low Moderate High

(values in database 4 3 2 1)

Factor 7 - Number and Variety of Interfaces Between the Project and Other Organizational Entities

General Descriptor

In the same way that a large number of different disciplines on a project can create a management challenge, a large number of different interfaces between organizations can as well.

Note: Issues of culture and language would be addressed here.

On the following four-point scale, please rate the number and variety of interfaces between the project and other organizational entities for each of the two projects you described.

Very Low Low Moderate High

(values in database 1 2 3 4)

Appendix G

Independent Samples T-Tests

Use of Practices by Public/Private Sector

Group Statistics

	Public/Private Sector	N	Mean	Std. Deviation	Std. Error Mean
Make Informed Decisions	Public	51	3.5163	.82277	.11521
	Private	89	3.9326	.67827	.07190
Build Support	Public	51	3.4804	.81216	.11373
	Private	89	3.6657	.67309	.07135
Manage Communications	Public	51	3.3129	.86209	.12072
	Private	89	3.7384	.80000	.08480
Engage Stakeholders	Public	51	3.2896	.79973	.11198
	Private	89	3.6885	.69477	.07365
Monitor and Control Progress	Public	49	3.1837	.98528	.14075
	Private	89	3.6695	.88758	.09408
Plan the Project	Public	51	3.1497	1.01754	.14248
	Private	89	3.6086	.85795	.09094
Manage Project Transitions	Public	50	2.9400	.98903	.13987
	Private	89	3.4869	.95882	.10163
Plan and Facilitate Change	Public	51	2.8745	1.13487	.15891
	Private	89	3.4674	1.10985	.11764
Ensure Business Integration	Public	51	2.8578	1.08478	.15190
	Private	89	3.4213	.99330	.10529
Prepare Users	Public	51	2.6881	1.11283	.15583
	Private	89	3.4867	1.13405	.12021
Communicate Change	Public	51	2.6993	1.06928	.14973
	Private	89	3.4532	1.17233	.12427
Evaluate and Improve Performance	Public	51	2.7902	1.04389	.14617
	Private	89	3.3112	.96147	.10192
Demonstrate Self-Awareness	Public	51	2.7908	.90667	.12696
	Private	88	3.2841	1.07037	.11410
Realize Benefits	Public	50	2.4350	1.14041	.16128
	Private	89	3.1910	1.16715	.12372

Independent Samples Test

		Levene's Test for Equality of Variances		T-Test for Equality of Means					95% Confidence Interval of the Difference	
		F	Sig.	t	df	Sig. (2-tailed)	Mean Difference	Std. Error Difference	Lower	Upper
Make Informed Decisions	Equal variances assumed	.044	.835	.848	138	.398	.11111	.13097	-.14785	.37008
	Equal variances not assumed			.841	114.318	.402	.11111	.13216	-.15069	.37291
Build Support	Equal variances assumed	.604	.438	1.666	138	.098	.20833	.12505	-.03892	.45559
	Equal variances not assumed			1.640	111.430	.104	.20833	.12707	-.04345	.46012
Manage Communications	Equal variances assumed	.162	.688	3.034	138	.003	.42999	.14173	.14975	.71023
	Equal variances not assumed			3.050	120.115	.003	.42999	.14099	.15084	.70913
Engage Stakeholders	Equal variances assumed	.081	.776	1.790	138	.076	.23189	.12954	-.02425	.48803
	Equal variances not assumed			1.769	113.105	.080	.23189	.13110	-.02784	.49163
Monitor and Control Progress	Equal variances assumed	.004	.952	1.073	136	.285	.17758	.16543	-.14958	.50474
	Equal variances not assumed			1.085	117.044	.280	.17758	.16373	-.14668	.50184
Plan the Project	Equal variances assumed	1.047	.308	1.462	138	.146	.23671	.16187	-.08336	.55677
	Equal variances not assumed			1.436	110.419	.154	.23671	.16489	-.09005	.56346
Manage Project Transitions	Equal variances assumed	.491	.485	1.383	137	.169	.23947	.17314	-.10290	.58184
	Equal variances not assumed			1.372	112.361	.173	.23947	.17458	-.10643	.58536
Plan and Facilitate Change	Equal variances assumed	.026	.872	3.068	138	.003	.59167	.19284	.21037	.97297
	Equal variances not assumed			3.065	117.627	.003	.59167	.19303	.20941	.97392
Ensure Business Integration	Equal variances assumed	.005	.941	2.592	138	.011	.46429	.17909	.11017	.81840
	Equal variances not assumed			2.588	117.372	.011	.46429	.17937	.10906	.81952
Prepare users	Equal variances assumed	2.710	.102	3.954	138	.000	.76995	.19474	.38489	1.15502
	Equal variances not assumed			4.076	129.391	.000	.76995	.18888	.39627	1.14364
Communicate Change	Equal variances assumed	.155	.695	3.967	138	.000	.77381	.19506	.38812	1.15950
	Equal variances not assumed			4.016	122.878	.000	.77381	.19267	.39243	1.15519
Evaluate and Improve Performance	Equal variances assumed	.015	.903	1.895	138	.060	.33036	.17436	-.01441	.67512
	Equal variances not assumed			1.895	118.048	.061	.33036	.17435	-.01490	.67562
Demonstrate Self-Awareness	Equal variances assumed	6.985	.009	1.868	137	.064	.33219	.17787	-.01955	.68392
	Equal variances not assumed			1.946	132.488	.054	.33219	.17072	-.00550	.66988
Realize Benefits	Equal variances assumed	.988	.322	3.112	137	.002	.63328	.20350	.23087	1.03569
	Equal variances not assumed			3.067	109.857	.003	.63328	.20649	.22405	1.04251

114

Use of Practices by Industry Sector

Group Statistics

	Industry Sector	N	Mean	Std. Deviation	Std. Error Mean
Make Informed Decisions	Finance and Services	84	3.8254	.74531	.08132
	Engineering	56	3.7143	.77961	.10418
Build Support	Finance and Services	84	3.6815	.70107	.07649
	Engineering	56	3.4732	.75930	.10147
Manage Communications	Finance and Services	84	3.7554	.82994	.09055
	Engineering	56	3.3254	.80867	.10806
Engage Stakeholders	Finance and Services	84	3.6359	.73262	.07994
	Engineering	56	3.4040	.77763	.10392
Monitor and Control Progress	Finance and Services	84	3.5665	.96559	.10535
	Engineering	54	3.3889	.92102	.12533
Plan the Projec+t	Finance and Services	84	3.5361	.90264	.09849
	Engineering	56	3.2994	.98963	.13225
Manage Project Transitions	Finance and Services	84	3.3849	.98243	.10719
	Engineering	55	3.1455	1.02191	.13779
Plan and Facilitate Change	Finance and Services	84	3.4881	1.11565	.12173
	Engineering	56	2.8964	1.12103	.14980 ·
Ensure Business Integration	Finance and Services	84	3.4018	1.03480	.11291
	Engineering	56	2.9375	1.04304	.13938
Prepare Users	Finance and Services	84	3.5038	1.19328	.13020
	Engineering	56	2.7338	1.02397	.13683
Communicate Change	Finance and Services	84	3.4881	1.15753	.12630
	Engineering	56	2.7143	1.08884	.14550
Evaluate and Improve Performance	Finance and Services	84	3.2536	1.01084	.11029
	Engineering	56	2.9232	1.01049	.13503
Demonstrate Self-Awareness	Finance and Services	83	3.2369	1.10864	.12169
	Engineering	56	2.9048	.89604	.11974
Realize Benefits	Finance and Services	84	3.1696	1.14015	.12440
	Engineering	55	2.5364	1.22230	.16482

Independent Samples Test

		Levene's Test for Equality of Variances		T-Test for Equality of Means					95% Confidence Interval of the Difference	
		F	Sig.	t	df	Sig. (2-tailed)	Mean Difference	Std. Error Difference	Lower	Upper
Make Informed Decisions	Equal variances assumed	.044	.835	.848	138	.398	.11111	.13097	-.14785	.37008
	Equal variances not assumed			.841	114.318	.402	.11111	.13216	-.15069	.37291
Build Support	Equal variances assumed	.604	.438	1.666	138	.098	.20833	.12505	-.03892	.45559
	Equal variances not assumed			1.640	111.430	.104	.20833	.12707	-.04345	.46012
Manage Communications	Equal variances assumed	.162	.688	3.034	138	.003	.42999	.14173	.14975	.71023
	Equal variances not assumed			3.050	120.115	.003	.42999	.14099	.15084	.70913
Engage Stakeholders	Equal variances assumed	.081	.776	1.790	138	.076	.23189	.12954	-.02425	.48803
	Equal variances not assumed			1.769	113.105	.080	.23189	.13110	-.02784	.49163
Monitor and Control Progress	Equal variances assumed	.004	.952	1.073	136	.285	.17758	.16543	-.14958	.50474
	Equal variances not assumed			1.085	117.044	.280	.17758	.16373	-.14668	.50184
Plan the Project	Equal variances assumed	1.047	.308	1.462	138	.146	.23671	.16187	-.08336	.55677
	Equal variances not assumed			1.436	110.419	.154	.23671	.16489	-.09005	.56346
Manage Project Transitions	Equal variances assumed	.491	.485	1.383	137	.169	.23947	.17314	-.10290	.58184
	Equal variances not assumed			1.372	112.361	.173	.23947	.17458	-.10643	.58536
Plan and Facilitate Change	Equal variances assumed	.026	.872	3.068	138	.003	.59167	.19284	.21037	.97297
	Equal variances not assumed			3.065	117.627	.003	.59167	.19303	.20941	.97392
Ensure Business Integration	Equal variances assumed	.005	.941	2.592	138	.011	.46429	.17909	.11017	.81840
	Equal variances not assumed			2.588	117.372	.011	.46429	.17937	.10906	.81952
Prepare Users	Equal variances assumed	2.710	.102	3.954	138	.000	.76995	.19474	.38489	1.15502
	Equal variances not assumed			4.076	129.391	.000	.76995	.18888	.39627	1.14364
Communicate Change	Equal variances assumed	.155	.695	3.967	138	.000	.77381	.19506	.38812	1.15950
	Equal variances not assumed			4.016	122.878	.000	.77381	.19267	.39243	1.15519
Evaluate and Improve Performance	Equal variances assumed	.015	.903	1.895	138	.060	.33036	.17436	-.01441	.67512
	Equal variances not assumed			1.895	118.048	.061	.33036	.17435	-.01490	.67562
Demonstrate Self-Awareness	Equal variances assumed	6.985	.009	1.868	137	.064	.33219	.17787	-.01955	.68392
	Equal variances not assumed			1.946	132.488	.054	.33219	.17072	-.00550	.66988
Realize Benefits	Equal variances assumed	.988	.322	3.112	137	.002	.63328	.20350	.23087	1.03569
	Equal variances not assumed			3.067	109.857	.003	.63328	.20649	.22405	1.04251

Use of Practices by Client Type

Group Statistics

	Client type	N	Mean	Std. Deviation	Std. Error Mean
Make Informed Decisions	External	34	4.0196	.46378	.07954
	Internal	106	3.7044	.81821	.07947
Build Support	External	34	3.6029	.72331	.12405
	Internal	106	3.5967	.73482	.07137
Manage Communications	External	34	3.4926	.74540	.12783
	Internal	106	3.6125	.87638	.08512
Engage Stakeholders	External	34	3.6171	.51566	.08844
	Internal	106	3.5194	.81996	.07964
Monitor and Control Progress	External	34	3.7794	.57985	.09944
	Internal	104	3.4046	1.02723	.10073
Plan the Project	External	34	3.5824	.77304	.13258
	Internal	106	3.3962	.98928	.09609
Manage Project Transitions	External	34	3.2941	.75996	.13033
	Internal	105	3.2889	1.07125	.10454
Plan and Facilitate Change	External	34	3.1235	1.09325	.18749
	Internal	106	3.2925	1.17114	.11375
Ensure Business Integration	External	34	3.2132	1.00214	.17187
	Internal	106	3.2170	1.08151	.10505
Prepare Users	External	34	3.1134	1.04729	.17961
	Internal	106	3.2222	1.23161	.11962
Communicate Change	External	34	3.0294	1.11424	.19109
	Internal	106	3.2264	1.21328	.11784
Evaluate and Improve Performance	External	34	3.2765	.92771	.15910
	Internal	106	3.0717	1.04724	.10172
Demonstrate Self-Awareness	External	34	3.2255	.88276	.15139
	Internal	105	3.0635	1.08417	.10580
Realize Benefits	External	34	2.6691	1.27136	.21804
	Internal	105	3.0000	1.18383	.11553

Independent Samples Test

		Levene's Test for Equality of Variances		T-Test for Equality of Means					95% Confidence Interval of the Difference	
		F	Sig.	t	df	Sig. (2-tailed)	Mean Difference	Std. Error Difference	Lower	Upper
Make Informed Decisions	Equal variances assumed	15.617	.000	2.136	138	.034	.31521	.14760	.02336	.60705
	Equal variances not assumed			2.803	100.347	.006	.31521	.11244	.09214	.53827
Build Support	Equal variances assumed	.001	.974	.043	138	.966	.00624	.14429	-.27906	.29155
	Equal variances not assumed			.044	56.519	.965	.00624	.14311	-.28039	.29288
Manage Communications	Equal variances assumed	.559	.456	-.718	138	.474	-.11985	.16692	-.44990	.21020
	Equal variances not assumed			-.780	64.751	.438	-.11985	.15358	-.42660	.18690
Engage Stakeholders	Equal variances assumed	6.937	.009	.654	138	.514	.09769	.14947	-.19786	.39324
	Equal variances not assumed			.821	89.691	.414	.09769	.11901	-.13875	.33414
Monitor and Control Progress	Equal variances assumed	15.028	.000	2.021	136	.045	.37476	.18540	.00812	.74140
	Equal variances not assumed			2.648	101.292	.009	.37476	.14155	.09398	.65554
Plan the Project	Equal variances assumed	3.472	.065	1.002	138	.318	.18613	.18568	-.18102	.55327
	Equal variances not assumed			1.137	70.649	.259	.18613	.16373	-.14038	.51263
Manage Project Transitions	Equal variances assumed	3.324	.070	.026	137	.979	.00523	.19833	-.38696	.39742
	Equal variances not assumed			.031	78.778	.975	.00523	.16708	-.32735	.33781
Plan and Facilitate Change	Equal variances assumed	.265	.607	-.743	138	.459	-.16892	.22725	-.61826	.28041
	Equal variances not assumed			-.770	59.242	.444	-.16892	.21930	-.60770	.26985
Ensure Business Integration	Equal variances assumed	.611	.436	-.018	138	.986	-.00375	.20952	-.41804	.41055
	Equal variances not assumed			-.019	59.645	.985	-.00375	.20143	-.40671	.39922
Prepare Users	Equal variances assumed	3.589	.060	-.464	138	.644	-.10879	.23457	-.57260	.35502
	Equal variances not assumed			-.504	64.766	.616	-.10879	.21580	-.53980	.32222
Communicate Change	Equal variances assumed	.525	.470	-.840	138	.403	-.19700	.23461	-.66090	.26689
	Equal variances not assumed			-.877	60.140	.384	-.19700	.22451	-.64606	.25205
Evaluate and Improve Performance	Equal variances assumed	1.182	.279	1.019	138	.310	.20477	.20102	-.19271	.60225
	Equal variances not assumed			1.084	62.223	.282	.20477	.18884	-.17268	.58223
Demonstrate Self-Awareness	Equal variances assumed	2.545	.113	.790	137	.431	.16200	.20506	-.24350	.56749
	Equal variances not assumed			.877	67.964	.384	.16200	.18470	-.20657	.53056
Realize Benefits	Equal variances assumed	1.693	.195	-1.391	137	.166	-.33088	.23787	-.80125	.13949
	Equal variances not assumed			-1.341	52.810	.186	-.33088	.24675	-.82585	.16408

Independent Samples Test

		Levene's Test for Equality of Variances		T-Test for Equality of Means					95% Confidence Interval of the Difference	
		F	Sig.	t	df	Sig. (2-tailed)	Mean Difference	Std. Error Difference	Lower	Upper
Make Informed Decisions	Equal variances assumed	15.852	.000	2.510	158	.013	.37581	.14975	.08004	.67159
	Equal variances not assumed			3.069	87.151	.003	.37581	.12247	.13239	.61924
Build Support	Equal variances assumed	.028	.867	.546	158	.586	.08104	.14833	-.21193	.37402
	Equal variances not assumed			.562	61.969	.576	.08104	.14427	-.20736	.36945
Manage Communications	Equal variances assumed	.552	.458	-.045	158	.964	-.00762	.16802	-.33947	.32423
	Equal variances not assumed			-.049	66.857	.961	-.00762	.15629	-.31959	.30435
Engage Stakeholders	Equal variances assumed	6.366	.013	1.268	158	.207	.19361	.15272	-.10802	.49524
	Equal variances not assumed			1.510	82.101	.135	.19361	.12821	-.06144	.44866
Monitor and Control Progress	Equal variances assumed	16.700	.000	2.449	156	.015	.44917	.18340	.08689	.81144
	Equal variances not assumed			3.149	99.858	.002	.44917	.14262	.16621	.73212
Plan the Project	Equal variances assumed	4.679	.032	1.258	158	.210	.22663	.18013	-.12915	.58241
	Equal variances not assumed			1.434	74.809	.156	.22663	.15799	-.08812	.54138
Manage Project Transitions	Equal variances assumed	4.632	.033	.475	157	.635	.09267	.19504	-.29257	.47792
	Equal variances not assumed			.569	83.734	.571	.09267	.16275	-.23099	.41634
Plan and Facilitate Change	Equal variances assumed	.069	.793	-.265	158	.792	-.05722	.21618	-.48418	.36975
	Equal variances not assumed			-.271	61.451	.788	-.05722	.21136	-.47980	.36536
Ensure Business Integration	Equal variances assumed	.329	.567	.525	158	.601	.10509	.20031	-.29054	.50071
	Equal variances not assumed			.537	61.586	.593	.10509	.19558	-.28592	.49609
Prepare Users	Equal variances assumed	2.479	.117	-.332	158	.741	-.07460	.22490	-.51879	.36959
	Equal variances not assumed			-.355	66.302	.724	-.07460	.21018	-.49421	.34501
Communicate Change	Equal variances assumed	.154	.695	-.324	158	.746	-.07237	.22329	-.51338	.36865
	Equal variances not assumed			-.332	61.530	.741	-.07237	.21814	-.50848	.36375
Demonstrate Self-Awareness	Equal variances assumed	1.622	.205	.858	157	.392	.16541	.19271	-.21523	.54605
	Equal variances not assumed			.937	69.054	.352	.16541	.17654	-.18677	.51759
Evaluate and Improve Performance	Equal variances assumed	.779	.379	1.331	158	.185	.25955	.19494	-.12548	.64457
	Equal variances not assumed			1.402	64.490	.166	.25955	.18511	-.11020	.62930
Realize Benefits	Equal variances assumed	.649	.422	-1.140	157	.256	-.26119	.22916	-.71382	.19144
	Equal variances not assumed			-1.119	57.896	.268	-.26119	.23342	-.72845	.20607

References

Aitken, A., & Crawford, L. H. (2007, September). A study of project categorisation based on project management complexity. *Proceedings of VIII IRNOP Conference*, Brighton, UK.

Aitken, A., & Crawford, L. H. (2008). Senior management perceptions of effective project manager behavior: An exploration of a core set of behaviors for superior project managers. *Proceedings of the PMI Research Conference*, Warsaw, Poland.

Anantatmula, V. S. (2010). Project manager leadership role in improving project performance. *Engineering Management Journal, 22*(1), 13–22.

Artto, K. A., Kulvik, I., Poskela, J., & Turkulainen, V. (2011). The integrative role of the project management office in the front end of innovation. *International Journal of Project Management, 29*(4), 408–421.

Artto, K. A., Martinsuo, M., Gemünden, H. G., & Murtoaro, J. (2009). Foundations of program management: A bibliometric view. *International Journal of Project Management, 27*(1), 1–18.

Ashley, D. B., Lurie, C. S., & Jaselskis, E. J. (1987). Determinants of construction project success. *Project Management Journal, 18*(2), 69–79.

Ashurst, C., & Hodges, J. (2010). Exploring business transformation: The challenges of developing a benefits realization capability. *Journal of Change Management, 10*(2), 217–237.

Association of Change Management Professionals (ACMP). (2012). You can always count on change in our profession. Retrieved from http://www.acmp.info/ACMP-news.asp. Washington, DC, ACMP.

Association for Project Management (APM). (2006). *APM body of knowledge* (5th ed.). High Wycombe: Association for Project Management.

Association for Project Management (APM). (2008). *APM competence framework*. High Wycombe: Association for Project Management.

Aubry, M., & Hobbs, J. B. (2011). A fresh look at the contribution of project management to organizational performance. *Project Management Journal, 42*(1), 3–16.

Aubry, M., Hobbs, J. B., & Thuillier, D. (2007). A new framework for understanding organisational project management through the PMO. *International Journal of Project Management, 25*(4), 328–336.

Aubry, M., Hobbs, J. B., & Thuillier, D. (2008). Organisational project management: An historical approach to the study of PMOs. *International Journal of Project Management, 26*(1), 38–43.

Aubry, M., Müller, R., Hobbs, J. B., & Blomquist, T. (2010). Project management offices in transition. *International Journal of Project Management*, *28*(8), 766–778.

Australian Institute of Project Management (AIPM). (2008, November). *AIPM professional competency standards for project management - Part C: Certified practising project manager (CPPM)* [Version 1.11]. Sydney, Australia: AIPM.

Australian Institute of Project Management (AIPM). (2011, January). *AIPM professional competency standards for project management - Part D: Certified practising project director (CPPD)* [Version 1.2]. Sydney, Australia: AIPM.

Baccarini, D. (1996). The concept of project complexity - A review. *International Journal of Project Management*, *14*(4), 201–204.

Baker, B. N., Murphy, D. C., & Fisher, D. (1988). Factors affecting project success. In D. I. Cleland & W. R. King (Eds.), *Project management handbook* (2nd ed., pp. 902–919). New York, NY: Van Nostrand Reinhold.

Balogun, J., & Hailey, V. H. (2008). *Exploring strategic change*. (3rd ed.). London, UK: Prentice Hall.

Bamford, D. R., & Forrester, P. L. (2003). Managing planned and emergent change within an operations management environment. *International Journal of Operations and Production Management*, *23*(5), 546–564.

Beale, P., & Freeman, M. (1991). Successful project execution: A model. *Project Management Journal*, *22*(4), 23–30.

Belassi, W., Kondra, A. Z., & Tukel, O. I. (2007). New product development projects: The effects of organizational culture. *Project Management Journal*, *38*(4), 12–24.

Belassi, W., & Tukel, O. I. (1996). A new framework for determining critical success/failure factors in projects. *International Journal of Project Management*, *14*(3), 141–151.

Beldi, A., Cheffi, W., & Dey, P. K. (2010). Managing customer relationship management projects: The case of a large French telecommunications company. *International Journal of Project Management*, *28*(4), 339–351.

Besner, C., & Hobbs, J. B. (2006). The perceived value and potential contribution of project management practices to project management success. *Project Management Journal*, *37*(3), 37–48.

Besner, C., & Hobbs, B. (2008). Project management practice, generic or contextual: A reality check. *Project Management Journal*, *39*(1), 16–33.

Besner, C., & Hobbs, J. B. (2011, June). Contextualised project management practice: A cluster analysis of practices and best practices. In IRNOP X Conference, Montreal, 19–22 June 2011 Montreal: University of Quebec at Montreal.

Betts, M., & Lansley, P. (1995). International Journal of Project Management: a review of the first ten years. *International Journal of Project Management*, *13*(4), 207–217.

Biedenbach, T., & Söderholm, A. (2008). The challenge of organizing change in hypercompetitive industries: A literature review. *Journal of Change Management*, *8*(2), 123–145.

Blichfeldt, B. S., & Eskerod, P. (2008). Project portfolio management - There's more to it than what management enacts. *International Journal of Project Management, 26*(4), 357–365.

Blomquist, T., & Müller, R. (2006). Practices, roles, and responsibilities of middle managers in program and portfolio management. *Project Management Journal, 37*(1), 52–66.

Bosch-Rekveldt, M., Jongkind, Y., Mooi, H., Bakker, H., & Verbraeck, A. (2011). Grasping project complexity in large engineering projects: The TOE (technical, organizational and environmental) framework. *International Journal of Project Management, 29*(6), 728–739.

Bosch-Rekveldt, M. G. C. (2011). Managing project complexity: A study into adapting early project phases to improve project performance in large engineering projects. Technical University of Delft, The Hague, The Netherlands.

Bresnen, M. (2006). Conflicting and conflated discourses? Project management, organisational change and learning. In D. E. Hodgson & S. J. K. Cicmil (Eds.), *Making projects critical* (68–89). New York, NY: Palgrave Macmillan.

British Standards Institution. (2010). BS 6079-1:2010: *Project management. Principles and guidelines for the management of projects.* London, England: British Standards Institution.

Brown, S. L., & Eisenhardt, K. M. (1997). The art of continuous change: Linking complexity theory and time-paced evolution in relentlessly shifting organizations. *Administrative Science Quarterly, 42*(1), 1–34.

Buchanan, D. A. (1991). Vulnerability and agenda: Context and process in project management. *British Journal of Management, 2*(3), 121–132.

Buchanan, D. A., & Boddy, D. (1992). *The expertise of the change agent.* In Prentice Hall.

Burnes, B. (2004a). Emergent change and planned change - competitors or allies? The case of XYZ construction. *International Journal of Operations & Production Management, 24*(9), 886–902.

Burnes, B. (2004b). Kurt Lewin and the planned approach to change: A re-appraisal. *Journal of Management Studies, 41*(6), 977–1002.

Burnes, B. (2004c). *Managing strategic change: A strategic approach to organizational dynamics.* Harlow, England: Prentice Hall.

By, R. T. (2005). Organisational change management: A critical review. *Journal of Change Management, 5*(4), 369–380.

By, R. T., & Macleod, C. (2009). *Managing organizational change in public services: international issues, challenges & cases.* London, UK: Routledge.

Caluwé, L. D., & Vermaak, H. (2003). *Learning to change: A guide for organisational change agents.* Thousand Oaks, CA: Sage Publications.

Cameron, K. S., & Quinn, R. E. (2005). Diagnosing and changing organizational culture: based on the competing values framework (Revised ed.). New York, NY: John Wiley.

Change Management Institute. (2008). Change Management Practitioner Competencies. [Online]. Retrieved from http://www.change-management-institute.com/Upload/CMI-Competency-Model-010408.pdf

Cheng, M.-I., & Dainty, A. R. J. (2005). What makes a good project manager? *Human Resource Management Journal, 15*(1), 25–37.

Christensen, D., & Walker, D. H. T. (2008). Using vision as a critical success element in project management. *International Journal of Managing Projects in Business, 1*(4), 611–622.

Cicmil, S. J. K. (1999). An insight into management of organisational change projects. *Journal of Workplace Learning, 11*(1), 5–15.

Cicmil, S. J. K., Cooke-Davies, T. J., Crawford, L. H., & Richardson, K. A. (2009). *Exploring the complexity of projects: Implications of complexity theory for project management practice.* Newtown Square, PA: Project Management Institute.

Cicmil, S. J. K., Williams, T., Thomas, J. L., & Hodgson, D. E. (2006). Rethinking project management: Researching the actuality of projects. *International Journal of Project Management, 24*(8), 675–686.

Clarke, A. (1995). The key success factors in project management. *Proceedings of a Teaching Company Seminar.* London, UK: The Teaching Company.

Clarke, A. (1999). A practical use of key success factors to improve the effectiveness of project management. *International Journal of Project Management, 17*(3), 139–145.

Cooke-Davies, T. J. (2001). Towards improved project management practice: Uncovering the evidence for effective practices through empirical research. USA: Dissertation.com.

Cooke-Davies, T. J. (2002). The "real" success factors on projects. *International Journal of Project Management, 2*(3), 185–190.

Cooke-Davies, T. J. (2004). Project success. In P. W. G. Morris & J. K. Pinto (Eds.), *The Wiley guide to managing projects.* Hoboken, NJ: John Wiley & Sons.

Cooke-Davies, T. J., & Arzymanow, A. (2003). The maturity of project management in different industries: An investigation into variations between project management models. Selected papers from the Fifth Biennial Conference of the International Research Network for Organizing by Projects. Held in Renesse, Seeland, The Netherlands, 28–31 May 2002. *International Journal of Project Management, 21*(6), 471–478.

Cooke-Davies, T. J., Cicmil, S. J. K., Crawford, L. H., & Richardson, K. (2007). We're not in Kansas anymore, Toto: Mapping the strange landscape of complexity theory, and its relationship to project management. *Project Management Journal, 38*(2), 50–61.

Cooke-Davies, T. J., Crawford, L. H., & Lechler, T. S. (2009). Project management systems: Moving project management from an operational to a strategic discipline. *Project Management Journal, 40*(1), 99–109.

Cooke-Davies, T. J., Crawford, L. H., Patton, J. R., Stevens, C., & Williams, T. M. (2011). *Aspects of complexity: Managing projects in a complex world*. Newtown Square, PA: Project Management Institute.

Cowan-Sahadath, K. (2010). Business transformation: Leadership, integration and innovation - A case study. *International Journal of Project Management, 28*(4), 395–404.

Crawford, L. H. (2001). *Project management competence: The value of standards*. (DBA Thesis ed.). Henley-on-Thames: Henley Management College/Brunel University.

Crawford, L. H. (2005). Senior management perceptions of project management competence. *International Journal of Project Management, 23*(1), 7–16.

Crawford, L. H. (2006). Developing organizational project management capability: Theory and practice. *Project Management Journal, 37*(3), 74–86.

Crawford, L. H., Aitken, A., & Hassner-Nahmias, A. (2011a, June). Embracing the implementation of change. Proceedings of X IRNOP Conference, Montreal, Quebec, Canada.

Crawford, L. H., Aitken, A., & Hassner-Nahmias, A. (2011b, June). Exploring the intersection of project and change management. Proceedings of EURAM (European Academy of Management) Conference, Estonia.

Crawford, L. H., & Cooke-Davies, T. J. (2012). *Best industry outcomes*. Newtown Square, PA: Project Management Institute.

Crawford, L. H., Costello, K. L., Pollack, J. B., & Bentley, L. (2003). Managing soft change projects in the public sector. *International Journal of Project Management, 21*(6), 443–448.

Crawford, L. H., & Hassner-Nahmias, A. (2010). Competencies for managing change. *International Journal of Project Management, 28*(4), 405–412.

Crawford, L. H., & Helm, J. (2009). Government and governance: The value of project management in the public sector. *Project Management Journal, 40*, 73–87.

Crawford, L. H., Hobbs, J. B., & Turner, J. R. (2005). *Project categorization systems: Aligning capability with strategy for better results*. Newtown Square, PA: Project Management Institute.

Crawford, L. H., Hobbs, J. B., & Turner, J. R. (2006). Aligning capability with strategy: Categorizing projects to do the right projects and to do them right. *Project Management Journal, 37*(2), 38–51.

Crawford, L. H., & Pollack, J. B. (2007). How generic are project management knowledge and practice? *Project Management Journal, 38*(1), 87–97.

Cummings, T. G., & Worley, C. G. (2001). *Organizational development and change* (7th ed.). Cincinnati, OH: South-Western College.

Davies, A., & Hobday, M. (2005). *The business of projects*. Cambridge, UK: Cambridge University Press.

Defence Materiel Organisation. (2004). Acquisition Categorisation Framework: Policy for the Categorisation of Programs and Projects. Canberra, ACT: Australian Government (Department of Defence).

Dietrich, P., & Lehtonen, P. (2005). Successful management of strategic intentions through multiple projects - Reflections from empirical study. *International Journal of Project Management, 23*(5), 386–391.

Dover, P. A. (2003). Change agents at work: Lessons from Siemens Nixdorf. *Journal of Change Management, 3*(3), 243–257.

Dunphy, D., & Stace, D. (1993). The strategic management of corporate change. *Human Relations, 46*(8), 905–920.

ECITB (2003). National Occupational Standards for Project Management Version 1.01. Kings Langley, Herts.: Engineering & Construction Industry Training Board.

Engwall, M. (2003). No project is an island: Linking projects to history and context. *Research Policy, 32*(5), 789–808.

Eskerod, P. (2010). Action learning for further developing project management competencies: A case study from an engineering consultancy company. *International Journal of Project Management, 28*(4), 352–360.

Eskerod, P., & Riis, E. (2009). Value creation by building an intra-organizational common frame of reference concerning project management. *Project Management Journal, 40*(3), 6–13.

Fiedler, S. (2010). Managing resistance in an organizational transformation: A case study from a mobile operator company. *International Journal of Project Management, 28*(4), 370–383.

Flyvbjerg, B., Bruzelius, N., & Rothengatter, W. (2003). *Megaprojects and risk: An anatomy of ambition.* Cambridge, UK: Cambridge University Press.

Fortune, J., & White, D. (2006). Framing of project critical success factors by a systems model. *International Journal of Project Management, 24*(1), 53–65.

French, W. L. & Bell, C. H. Jr. (1999). Organization development: Behavioral science interventions for organization improvement. Upper Saddle River, NJ: Prentice Hall.

Gareis, R. (2010). Changes of organizations by projects. *International Journal of Project Management, 28*(4), 314–327.

Gareis, R., & Huemann, M. (2008). Change management and projects. *International Journal of Project Management, 26*, 771–772.

Gareis, R., & Huemann, M. (2010). Guest editorial. *International Journal of Project Management, 28*(4), 311–313.

Geddes, M. (1990). Project leadership and the involvement of users in IT projects. *International Journal of Project Management, 8*(4), 214–216.

Geoghegan, L., & Dulewicz, V. (2008). Do project managers' leadership competencies contribute to project success? *Project Management Journal, 39*(4), 58–67.

Geraldi, J. G. (2008). The balance between order and chaos in multi-project firms: A conceptual model. *International Journal of Project Management, 26*(4), 348–356.

Global Alliance for Project Performance Standards. (2007). *A framework for performance based competency standards for global level 1 and 2 project managers.* Johannesburg: Global Alliance for Project Performance Standards.

Global Alliance for Project Performance Standards. (2011). *A framework for performance based competency standards for program managers.* Sydney: Global Alliance for Project Performance Standards.

Gonczi, A., Hager, P., & Athanasou, J. (1993). *The development of competency-based assessment strategies for the professions.* Canberra, Australia: Australian Government Publishing Service.

Graetz, F., Rimmer, M., Smith, A., & Lawrence, A. (2006). *Managing organizational change.* (2nd ed.). Milton, Australia: John Wiley & Sons.

Graetz, F., & Smith, A. C. T. (2011). Managing organizational change: A philosophies of change approach. *Journal of Change Management, 10*(2), 135–154.

Griffith-Cooper, B., & King, K. (2007). The partnership between project management and organizational change: Integrating change management with change leadership. *Performance Improvement, 46*(1), 14–20.

Hammer, M., & Champy, J. (1993). *Reengineering the corporation.* London, UK: Nicholas Brealey Publishing.

Hassner-Nahmias, A. (2009). Who is the change manager? PhD Thesis Bond University, Gold Coast, Australia.

Hassner-Nahmias, A., & Crawford, L. H. (2008). Project manager or change manager? Who should be managing organizational change? *Proceedings of the PMI Research Conference,* Warsaw, Poland. Newtown Square, PA: Project Management Institute.

Higgs, M., & Rowland, D. (2000). Building change leadership capability: 'The quest for competence.' *Journal of Change Management, 1*(2), 116–130.

Higgs, M., & Rowland, D. (2005). All changes great and small: Exploring approaches to change and its leadership. *Journal of Change Management, 5*(2), 121–152.

Hobbs, J. B., Aubry, M., & Thuillier, D. (2008). The project management office as an organisational innovation. *International Journal of Project Management, 26*(5), 547–555.

Huemann, M. (2010). Considering human resource management when developing a project-oriented company: Case study of a telecommunication company. *International Journal of Project Management, 28*(4), 361–369.

Huemann, M., Keegan, A., & Turner, J. R. (2007). Human resource management in the project-oriented company: A review. *International Journal of Project Management, 25*(3), 315–323.

Huemann, M., Turner, J. R., & Keegan, A. E. (2004). The role of human resource management in project-oriented organizations. In D. P. Slevin, D. I. Cleland, & J. K. Pinto (Eds.), *Proceedings of the 2004 PMI Research Conference,* London, UK. Newtown Square, PA: Project Management Institute.

IBSA (2009). BSB51407 Diploma of Project Management. Melbourne: Innovation and Business Skills Australia / Commonwealth of Australia.

Ika, L. A. (2009). Project success as a topic in project management journals. *Project Management Journal, 40*(4), 6–19.

Iles, V., & Sutherland, K. (2001). Managing Change in the NHS : Organisational Change - A Review for Health Care Managers, Professionals and Researchers. London, UK: National Co-ordinating Centre for NHS Service Delivery and Organisation Research and Development (accessible in July 2010 through http://www.sdo.nihr.ac.uk/managing change.html).

International Institute of Business Analysis. (2009). A guide to the business analysis body of knowledge® (BABOK® Guide) Version 2.0. Toronto, Canada: International Institute of Business Analysis.

International Institute of Business Analysis. (2011). IIBA(R) Business Analysis Competency Model Version 3.0. Toronto, Canada: International Institute of Business Analysis.

International Project Management Association. (2006). ICB - IPMA Competence Baseline Version 3.0. Nijkerk, The Netherlands: International Project Management Association.

Ismail, W. K. W., Nor, K. M., & Marjani, T. (2009). The role of knowledge sharing practice in enhancing project success. *Interdisciplinary Journal of Contemporary Research in Business, 1*(7), 34.

Jiang, J. J., Klein, G., & Balloun, J. (1996). Ranking of system implementation success factors. *Project Management Journal, 27*(4), 49–53.

Jugdev, K., Mathur, G., & Fung, T. S. (2007). Project management assets and their relationship with the project management capability of the firm. *International Journal of Project Management, 25*(6), 560–568.

Jugdev, K., & Müller, R. (2005). A retrospective look at our evolving understanding of project success. *Project Management Journal, 36*(4), 19–31.

Kanter, R. M., Stein, B. A., & Jick, T. D. (1992). *The challenge of organizational changes.* New York, NY: The Free Press.

Kliem, R. L., Ludin, I. S., & Robertson, K. L. (1997). *Project management methodology, A practical guide for the millennium.* New York, NY: Marcel Dekker.

Kloppenborg, T. J., & Opfer, W. A. (2000, June). Forty years of project management research: Trends, interpretations, and predictions. In Project Management Research at the Turn of the Millenium: *Proceedings of PMI Research Conference,* Paris, France (pp. 41–59). Sylva, NC: Project Management Institute.

Kotter, J. P. (1996). *Leading change.* Boston, MA: Harvard Business School Press.

Kotter, J. P. & Schlesinger, L. A. (2008). Choosing strategies for change. *Harvard Business Review, 86*(7/8), 130–139.

Lechler, T. S. (1998). When it comes to project management, it's the people that matter: An empirical analysis of project management in Germany. In F. Hartman, G. Jergeas, & J. L. Thomas (Eds.), The nature and role of projects in the next

20 years: Research issues and problems. Proceedings of III IRNOP Conference, Calgary, Alberta, Canada (pp. 205–215).

Lechler, T. S., & Byrne, J. C. (2010). *The mindset for creating value.* Newtown Square, PA: Project Management Institute.

Lehmann, V. (2010). Connecting changes to projects using a historical perspective: Towards some new canvases for researchers. *International Journal of Project Management, 28*(4), 328–338.

Lehtonen, P., & Martinsuo, M. (2008). Change program initiation: Defining and managing the program-organization boundary. *International Journal of Project Management, 26*(1), 21–29.

Levasseur, R. E. (2010). People skills: Ensuring project success—a change management perspective. *Interfaces, 40*(2), 159–162.

Levene, R., & Braganza, A. (1996). Controlling the work scope in organisational transformation: A programme management approach: Business process re-engineering and beyond. *International Journal of Project Management, 14*(6), 331–339.

Levy, A., & Merry, U. (1986). *Organizational transformation: approaches, strategies, theories.* New York, NY: Praeger.

Lewin, K. (1951). *Field theory in social sciences.* New York, NY: Harper and Row.

Leybourne, S. A. (2007). The changing bias of project management research: a consideration of the literatures and an application of extant theory. *Project Management Journal, 38*(1), 61–73.

Leybourne, S. (2006). Improvisation within the project management of change: Some observations from UK financial services. *Journal of Change Management, 6*(4), 365–381.

Lim, C. S., & Mohamed, M. Z. (1999). Criteria of project success: An exploratory re-examination. *International Journal of Project Management, 17*(4), 243–248.

Luo, J. S., Hilty, D. M., Worley, L. L., & Yager, J. (2006). Considerations in change management related to technology. *Academic Psychiatry, 30*(6), 465–469.

Lycett, M., Rassau, A., & Danson, J. (2004). Programme management: A critical review. *International Journal of Project Management, 22*(4), 289–299.

Maguire, S., & Redman, T. (2007). The role of human resources management in information systems development. *Management Decision, 45*(2), 252–264.

Malach-Pines, A., Dvir, D., & Sadeh, A. (2009). Project manager-project (PM-P) fit and project success. *International Journal of Operations & Production Management, 29*(3), 268–291.

Martin, W. (2011). Critical success factors of shared service projects - Results of an empirical study. *Advances in Management, 4*(5), 21–26.

Martinsuo, M., & Lehtonen, P. (2007). Program and its initiation in practice: Development program initiation in a public consortium: European Academy of Management (EURAM 2006) Conference. *International Journal of Project Management, 25*(4), 337–345.

Maylor, H., Brady, T., Cooke-Davies, T. J., & Hodgson, D. E. (2006). From projectification to programmification: Rethinking Project Management. *International Journal of Project Management, 24*(8), 663–674.

Meredith, J. R., & Mantel, S. J. Jr. (1995). *Project management: A managerial approach*. (3rd ed.). New York, NY: John Wiley & Sons, Inc.

Miller, R., & Lessard, D. R. (2001). *The strategic management of large engineering projects: Shaping institutions, risks and governance*. Cambridge, MA: The MIT Press.

Milosevic, D. Z., & Srivannaboon, S. (2006). A theoretical framework for aligning project management with business strategy. *Project Management Journal, 37,* 98–110.

Moran, J. W. & Brightman, B. K. (2001). Leading organizational change. *Career Development International 6*(2), 111–119.

Morris, P. W. G. (2002). Research trends in the 1990s: The need to focus on business benefit of project management. In D. P. Slevin, D. I. Cleland, & J. K. Pinto (Eds.), *The frontiers of project management research* (pp. 31–56). Newtown Square, Pennsylvania: Project Management Institute.

Morris, P. W. G., Crawford, L. H., Hodgson, D. E., Shepherd, M. M., & Thomas, J. L. (2006). Exploring the role of formal bodies of knowledge in defining a discipline/profession. *International Journal of Project Management, 24*(8), 710–721.

Morris, P. W. G., & Hough, G. H. (1993). *The anatomy of major projects*. Chichester, UK: John Wiley & Sons.

Morris, P. W. G., & Jamieson, A. (2005). Moving from corporate strategy to project strategy. *Project Management Journal, 36*(4), 5–18.

Morris, P. W. G., Patel, M. B., & Wearne, S. H. (2000). Research into revising the APM project management body of knowledge. *International Journal of Project Management, 18*(3), 155–164.

Morris, P. W. G., & Pinto, J. K. (2004). *The Wiley guide to managing projects*. Hoboken, NJ: John Wiley & Sons.

Müller, R., Geraldi, J., & Turner, J. R. (2012). Relationships between leadership and success in different types of project complexities. *IEEE Transactions on Engineering Management, 59*(1), 77–90.

Müller, R., & Turner, J. R. (2007a). Matching the project manager's leadership style to project type. *International Journal of Project Management, 25*(1), 21–32.

Müller, R., & Turner, J. R. (2007b). The influence of project managers on project success criteria and project success by type of project. *European Management Journal, 25*(4), 298–309.

Murphy, D. C., Baker, B. N., & Fisher, D. (1974). Determinants of project success. Boston: Boston College, National Aeronautics and Space Administration.

National Aeronautics and Space Administration. (2008). Academy of Program/ Project & Engineering Leadership. [On-line]. from http://appel.nasa.gov

Nicholas, J., & Hidding, G. (2010). Management principles associated with IT project success. *International Journal of Management and Information Systems*, *14*(5), 147–156.

Nieminen, A., & Lehtonen, M. (2008). Organisational control in programme teams: An empirical study in change programme context. *International Journal of Project Management*, *26*(1), 63–72.

Nikolaou, I., Gouras, A., Vakola, M., & Bourantis, D. (2007). Selecting change agents: Exploring traits and skills in a simulated environment. *Journal of Change Management*, *7*(3–4), 291–313.

Obeng, E. (1994). All Change! The Project Leader's Secret Handbook. London, UK: Pitman Publishing.

Office of Government Commerce (OGC). (2004). Successful delivery skills framework, Version 3.0. www.ogc.gov.uk: OGC.

Office of Government Commerce (OGC). (2007). *Managing Successful Programmes*. (3rd ed.). London: TSO (The Stationery Office).

Office of Government Commerce (OGC). (2008) *About the Office of Government Commerce*. Retrieved on November 21, 2008 from http://www.ogc.gov.uk.

Office of Government Commerce (2009). Managing successful projects with PRINCE2. London: TSO.

Oswick, C., & Robertson, M. (2009). Boundary objects reconsidered: From bridges and anchors to barricades and mazes. *Journal of Change Management*, *9*(2), 179–193.

Pandza, K., & Thorpe, R. (2009). Creative search and strategic sense-making: Missing dimensions in the concept of dynamic capabilities. *British Journal of Management*, *20*(S1), S118–S131.

Partington, D. (1996). The project management of organizational change. *International Journal of Project Management*, *14*(1), 13–21.

Partington, D., Pellegrinelli, S., & Young, M. (2005). Attributes and levels of programme management competence: an interpretive study. *International Journal of Project Management*, *23*(2), 87–89.

Partington, D., Young, M., & Pellegrinelli, S. (2003). Understanding program management competence: A phenomenographic study. *Academy of Management Proceedings* (pp. B1–B6).

Patanakul, P., Iewwongcharoen, B., & Milosevic, D. Z. (2010). An empirical study on the use of project management tools and techniques across project life-cycle and their impact on project success. *Journal of General Management*, *35*(3), 41–65.

Pellegrinelli, S. (1997). Programme management: Organising project-based change. *International Journal of Project Management*, *15*(3), 141–149.

Pellegrinelli, S. (2002). Shaping context: The role and challenge for programmes. *International Journal of Project Management, 20*(3), 229–233.

Pellegrinelli, S., Partington, D., Hemingway, C., Mohdzain, Z., & Shah, M. (2007). The importance of context in programme management: An empirical review of programme practices. *International Journal of Project Management, 25*(1), 41–55.

Penrose, E. T. (1959). *Theory of the growth of the firm.* New York, NY: Wiley.

Peppard, J., & Ward, J. (2004). Beyond strategic information systems: Towards an IS capability. *Journal of Strategic Information Systems, 13*(2), 167–194.

Pettigrew, A. M., McKee, L., & Ferlie, E. (1992). *Shaping strategic change: Making change in large organizations: The case of the National Health Service.* London, UK: Sage Publications.

Pinto, J. K. (2006). *Project management: Achieving competitive advantage.* Hoboken, NJ: John Wiley.

Pinto, J. K., & Covin, J. G. (1989). Critical factors in project implementation: A comparison of construction and R&D projects. *Technovation, 9*(1), 49–62.

Pinto, J. K., & Slevin, D. P. (1987). Critical factors in successful project implementation. *IEEE Transactions on Engineering Management,* EM-34, 22–27.

Pinto, J. K., & Slevin, D. P. (1988). Project success: Definitions and measurement techniques. *Project Management Journal, 19*(3), 67–72.

Piyush, M., Dangayach, G. S., & Mittal, M. L. (2011). A study of critical project success parameters in different organizational conditions. *Advances in Management, 4*(8), 50–56.

Project Management Institute. (2004). *A guide to the project management body of knowledge (PMBOK® guide)* (3rd ed.). Newtown Square, PA: Project Management Institute.

Project Management Institute. (2007). *Project manager competency development (PMCD) framework.* Newtown Square, PA: Project Management Institute.

Project Management Institute. (2008a). *A guide to the project management body of knowledge (PMBOK® guide)* (4th ed.). Newtown Square, PA: Project Management Institute.

Project Management Institute. (2008b). *The standard for program management* (2nd ed.) Newtown Square, PA: Project Management Institute.

Quinn, R. E. (1996). *Deep change.* San Francisco, CA: Jossey-Bass.

Quinn, R. E. (2004). *Building the bridge as you walk on it*: *A guide for leading change.* San Francisco, CA: Jossey-Bass.

Rai, A., Maruping, L. M., & Venkatesh, V. (2009). Offshore information systems project success: The role of social embeddedness and cultural characteristics. *MIS Quarterly, 33*(3), 617–641.

Remington, K. (2011). *Leading complex projects.* Farnham, Surrey, UK: Gower Publishing Limited.

Remington, K., & Pollack, J. B. (2007). *Tools for complex projects.* Aldershot, UK: Gower.

Riddell, P., & Haddon, C. (2009). *Transitions: Preparing for changes in government.* London, UK: Institute for Government.

Sahlin-Andersson, K., & Söderholm, A. (2002). The Scandinavian school of project studies. In K. Sahlin-Andersson & A. Söderholm (Eds.), *Beyond project management: New perspectives on the temporary - permanent dilemma* (pp. 11–24). Malmo, Sweden: Copenhagen Business School Press.

SAQA (2010). National Diploma: Project Management NQF Level 05. South Africa: South African Qualifications Authority.

Self, D. R., Armenakis, A. A., & Schraeder, M. (2007). Organizational change content, process and context: A simultaneous analysis of employee reactions. *Journal of Change Management, 7*(2), 211–229.

Shenhar, A. J. (2004). Strategic project leadership: Toward a strategic approach to project management. *R&D Management, 34*(5), 569–578.

Shenhar, A. J., & Dvir, D. (1996). Toward a typological theory of project management. *Research Policy, 25*(4), 607–632.

Sirkin, H. L., Keenan, P., & Jackson, A. (2005). The hard side of change management. *Harvard Business Review, 83*, 108–118.

Slevin, D. P., & Pinto, J. K. (1986). The project implementation profile: New tool for project managers. *Project Management Journal, 17*, 57–70.

Söderlund, J. (2010). Knowledge entrainment and project management: The case of large-scale transformation projects. *International Journal of Project Management, 28*(2), 130–141.

Söderlund, J., & Tell, F. (2009). The P-form organization and the dynamics of project competence: Project epochs in Asea/ABB, 1950–2000. *International Journal of Project Management, 27*(2), 101–112.

Srivannaboon, S., & Milosevic, D. Z. (2006). A two-way influence between business strategy and project management. *International Journal of Project Management, 24*(6), 493–505.

Stacey, R. D. (2001). *Complex responsive processes in organizations: Learning and knowledge creation.* New York, NY: Routledge.

Stummer, M., & Zuchi, D. (2010). Developing roles in change processes - A case study from a public sector organisation. *International Journal of Project Management, 28*(4), 384–394.

Tan, W.-G., Cater-Steel, A., & Toleman, M. (2009). Implementing IT service management: A case study focusing on critical success factors. *International Association for Computer Information Systems, 50*(2), 1–12.

Teece, D. J. (2009). *Dynamic capabilities and strategic management: Organizing for innovation and growth.* Oxford, UK: Oxford University Press.

Teece, D. J., Pisano, G., & Shuen, A. (1997). Dynamic capabilities and strategic management. *Strategic Management Journal, 18*(7), 509–533.

Thi, C. H., & Swierczek, F. W. (2010). Critical success factors in project management: Implication from Vietnam. *Asia Pacific Business Review, 16*(4), 567–589.

Thomas, J. L., & Buckle-Henning, P. (2007). Dancing in the white spaces: Exploring gendered assumptions in successful project managers' discourse about their work. *International Journal of Project Management, 25*(6), 552–559.

Thomas, J. L., & Mullaly, M. E. (2005). What's the benefit? Challenges in demonstrating the value of project management. *Proceedings of PMI North American Global Congress.* Newtown Square, PA: Project Management Institute.

Thomas, J. L., & Mullaly, M. E. (2008). *Researching the value of project management.* Newtown Square, PA: Project Management Institute.

Turner, J. R., & Cochrane, R. A. (1993). Goals-and-methods matrix: Coping with projects with ill defined goals and/or methods of achieving them. *International Journal of Project Management, 11*(2), 93–112.

Turner, J. R., Grude, K. V., & Thurloway, L. (1996). *The project manager as change agent: leadership influence and negotiation.* London, UK: McGraw-Hill.

Turner, J. R., & Müller, R. (2003). On the nature of the project as a temporary organization. *International Journal of Project Management, 21*(1), 1–8.

U.K. Cabinet Office. (2011). Managing successful programmes. London, UK: TSO (The Stationery Office).

Wateridge, J. F. (1996). Delivering successful IS/IT projects: Eight key elements from success criteria to review via appropriate management, methodologies and teams. Henley Management College, Brunel University.

Weick, K. E. (2001). *Making sense of the organization.* Malden, MA: Blackwell Publishing.

Weick, K. E., & Quinn, R. E. (1999). Organisational change and development. *Annual Review of Psychology, 50,* 361–386.

Westerveld, E. (2003). The project excellence model®: Linking success criteria and critical success factors. *International Journal of Project Management, 21*(6), 411–418.

Whittington, R., Molloy, E., Mayer, M., & Smith, A. (2006). Practices of strategising/organising: Broadening strategy work and skills. *Long Range Planning, 39*(6), 615–629.

Williams, T. M. (2002). *Modelling complex projects.* Chichester, UK: New York: Wiley.

Winter, M. C., Anderson, E. S., Elvin, R., & Levene, R. J. (2006). Focusing on business projects as an area for future research: An exploratory discussion of four different perspectives. *International Journal of Project Management, 24*(8), 699–709.

Winter, M. C., Smith, C., Morris, P. W. G., & Cicmil, S. J. K. (2006). Directions for future research in project management: The main findings of the EP-

SRC research network. *International Journal of Project Management, 24*(8), 638–649.

Yazici, H. J. (2009). The role of project management maturity and organizational culture in perceived performance. *Project Management Journal, 40*(3), 14–33.

Zahra, S. A., Sapienza, H. J., & Davidsson, P. (2006). Entrepreneurship and dynamic capabilities: A review, model and research agenda. *Journal of Management Studies, 43*(4), 917–955.

Zimmerer, T. W., & Yasin, M. M. (1998). A leadership profile of American project managers. *Project Management Journal, 29*(1), 31–38.

Zwikael, O. (2009). The relative importance of the PMBOK® guide's nine knowledge areas during project planning. *Project Management Journal, 40*(4), 94–103.

Zwikael, O., & Globerson, S. (2006). From critical success factors to critical success processes. *International Journal of Production Research, 44*(17), 3433–3449.